The Transportation Renaissance

The Transportation

Renaissance

The Personal Rapid
Transit Solution

Edmund W F Rydell

To order additional copies of this book, contact:
Xlibris Corporation
1-888-7-XLIBRIS
www.Xlibris.com
Orders@Xlibris.com

Contents

To all those who have gone before, and given of their
lives to achieve this dream;

to those of the present, who are the shepherds of the
world's finest transportation technology;

and to those of the future, on whose shoulders will rest the
design of vast networks
which we can hardly imagine.

Acknowledgments

This book could not have been written without the generous help of Dr. J. Edward Anderson. In a way, it is *his* book; without the many documents he furnished which provided most of the information, it would not have been possible to produce it. These include his documentary, *Some Early History of Personal Rapid Transit, Some Lessons from the History of PRT*, various pamphlets and expositions, as well as many of his over 90 published papers.

The germ of the idea came one evening in the fall of 1999 when visiting at his home. I remarked that, although we had his ground-breaking textbook, *Transit Systems Theory*, and his published papers on PRT, as well as texts by others, we really had no single book which popularized PRT and made it understandable to the public.

He responded by saying, "Well, you've written several books, you're an author; why don't you write it?"

Thus was born the concept. Dr. Anderson also came up with the title that same evening, which was immediately accepted by all present.

I am also indebted to Bob Fillmore, an engineer who worked on the Morgantown project. With his contribution, the chapter on Morgantown is, I believe, the most comprehensive description of the Morgantown fiasco yet published.

Another important name is that of Dr. Jarold A. Kieffer. His introduction to this book is a classic statement about advanced transportation. This book would be glaringly incomplete if it failed to mention the critical role Dr. Kieffer has played throughout much of the development history of PRT. His stature is such that it warranted the devotion of an entire chapter to his contribution.

26-RYDE

The warm, personal letters which he graciously provided contributed much to both the manuscript itself and to the furtherance of my understanding. Upon proof reading the manuscript, he submitted many corrections and pieces of information which were so lucidly written than I simply lifted them verbatim for use in the text. I am greatly in his debt.

Catherine G. Burke's scholarly work, *Innovation and Public Policy*, with the subtitle of *The Case of PRT*, was highly instrumental in furthering my understanding. Her detailing of the bungling of government agencies puts the blame squarely where it belongs, even though her criticisms are restrained and, if anything, quite gentle. Her work is highly recommended as additional reading.

I am indebted to A. Scheffer Lang, Chairman of the Board of Taxi 2000 and one of the outstanding spark plugs of the PRT movement, for providing details of the history of the American railroads in establishing a uniform track gauge (chapter 13). He also reviewed and made valuable suggestions relative to this chapter.

I thankfully acknowledge the careful evaluation of the text by my faithful proofreader, Dorothy Politis. Her numerous corrections in English grammar and usage and general readability were indispensable.

Finally, I am grateful to the Xlibris Corporation for providing a unique publishing service ideally suited to this book, and for the fine cooperation of their staff.

$\mathcal{I}$ntroduction

Worldwide, metropolitan areas are continuing to spread out and are dominated by medium and lower density types of development. In most of these places, public transit services are too expensive in their construction and operating costs to allow transit expansions to keep up with the rapid diffusion of their populations. Even, in some of the older central cities, where transit services were fairly diffused, transit has been losing market share to automobiles. However, as auto use continues to mushroom, roads are increasingly clogged, air pollution has suffered, road-building costs are going up, and public antagonism is growing against the taking of more and more land for road expansions and parking. At the same time, lack of effective transit service also is deepening the mobility problems of the rapidly expanding population over age 75, persons with disabilities, and many lower income people whose labor force participation and access to services is inhibited by the lack of effective transportation.

Transportation and urban planners project that continued population growth and economic development will bring even higher—much higher—levels of vehicular traffic on the roads. In many communities, congestion already is already into the crisis stage, with added road lanes providing ever shorter periods of relief. Mounting traffic congestion on the one hand and lack of effective mobility for large numbers of people on the other may prove to be the achilles heel in terms of the economics and effective functioning of the modern metropolitan area. Current conventional transit modes—heavy and light rail and buses—have

11

shown no promise of coping with or even easing today's traffic congestion, yet alone what is projected. The seriously limited role of these modes is the result of their high costs and operating requirements.

These conditions and the threats they present cry out for new thinking and action that would be responsive to the challenge. The focus of such new thinking and action must be the further development and practical deployment of more service-effective off-the-road modes of transit that could be low enough in cost to permit over time their widespread deployment in the medium/lower density areas.

Why has public policy at all levels failed to push hard for such transit alternatives that could head off unmanageable increases in road congestion and give greater mobility to people now denied it?

In so many modern areas of endeavor, both private and public policies and private initiatives and investments have fostered new, advanced technologies and processes designed to broaden service, improve quality, increase productivity, and lower costs. Indeed, such innovative endeavors have revolutionized the way we communicate and share information, the ways we do business, the ways we design and test products, the ways we merchandise, and the ways we provide services—but not public transportation services!

Even most of the newer automated guideway transit modes have proved, worldwide, to be too costly for more than limited use along a few corridors, or they serve a few activity centers. For these reasons, they could not be responsive to the main transit challenge of the metropolitan areas, for widely diffused transit service, and, indeed, were not designed to respond to it.

The inexplicable neglect of this challenge by public policy at all levels and private capital is the bad news! The good news is that, notwithstanding, a great amount of developmental work has been done on transit modes that could meet the transit challenge of the metropolitan areas. This book, by Edmund Rydell, has as its purpose the illumination of one of these concepts, namely, personal rapid transit, and the pioneer work on its conception by Donn Fichter, Jack Irving, and J. Edward Anderson, and others. The book also develops the role of the Advanced Transit Association, a not-for-profit educational organization that has for over a generation sought to encourage public and private interest in the need for more service-effective and much more cost-effective public transportation for the world's rapidly expanding metropolitan areas.

The message of this book and its focus on the new thinking and action so greatly needed in metropolitan area transportation could not be more timely.

Jarold A. Kieffer
Former Chairman
Advanced Transit Association

Chapter 1

Personal and Impersonal Modes

The twenty-first century will witness a dramatic change in the public transportation industry, a veritable Renaissance, a flowering of a new technology. The change is long overdue. While other fields have enjoyed striking changes which are entirely new, the transportation industry has had to be content with only improvements.

Transportation systems can be classified into two modes, personal and impersonal. Examples of personal modes are the automobile and the taxicab. For individuals, one should also include bicycles and motorcycles, and, reaching back into history, the rickshaw, and even horse-drawn carriages and horses or donkeys. In personal transport, trips are usually made without stops to pick up or drop off other persons. Examples of impersonal transportation modes are railroads, streetcars, busses, subways, monorails and light rail. In these modes, a fixed course is traveled, and vehicles stop frequently to let passengers board or get off. Thus the first observation that can be drawn is that personal transportation has been with us since antiquity, but impersonal transportation is the product of the industrial age.

Personal transportation is directly concerned with fulfilling the needs of the individual passenger. Impersonal transportation is not concerned with the individual passenger, only with passengers as an undifferentiated whole. Personal transportation has the objective of minimizing the decisions a passenger must make, and the frustrations which often accompany such decisions. Impersonal

15

transportation does not concern itself with these objectives. Thus, for example, a passenger using impersonal transportation must be alert and watching for the proper place to get off. The system will not do this for him. This can be quite agonizing in a unfamiliar city, in which the destination is hardly known or barely recognizable. Bus drivers are sometimes helpful but this can still be a problem, particularly in a foreign country if there is a language barrier.

A user of impersonal transportation must also learn, for example, which bus route to use, which bus to take, and how to recognize it; or which train to take on which track. This is not a problem for a commuter taking the same bus or train every day, but for others it can be nerve-racking.

In contrast, personal transportation such as a taxicab eliminates these problems. The passenger need only know his destination. Such service comes at relatively high cost, and sometimes one suspects that his cab driver is not taking the route which may be the most direct.

The automobile, being more comfortable, convenient, and safe is more appropriate to the discussion than other forms of personal transportation such as the bicycle and the motorcycle. The personal transportation of the automobile eliminates most of the problems of impersonal transportation, but it is relatively expensive when all factors are considered. It also introduces more problems of its own. One must still choose the best route, and increasingly that has come to mean a route which may not be the most direct, but which is more likely to avoid heavy traffic. When the destination is reached, the problem of what to do with the car arises. In just the last decade parking has mushroomed from being a small annoyance into being a major problem and expense. Once parked, the final destination may still entail quite a walk.

These shortcomings notwithstanding, personal forms of transportation are clearly much preferred by the general public over impersonal forms. Many studies have shown this, but the unimpressive ridership figures on practically all forms of public transportation confirm this conclusion without question. Despite the disadvantages, the automobile remains king. Most of us still prefer the convenience and directness of our cars to any other form of transportation.

Chapter 2

A Wish List

If we could ask anything we wanted of a completely new transportation technology, a sort of wish list of features, no matter how unlikely of attainment, and price being no object, what would be the parameters we would want? Such a list is not difficult to compile. It is clear that the new technology would have to produce a system that was personal, rather than impersonal. In fact, the features of the taxicab are an excellent guide in producing such a list, but it is far from complete. Here are features most of us would probably desire:

The only thing a passenger should need to know is his destination.

The vehicle should not make any stops of any kind until it delivers the passenger at his chosen destination.

He should never have to transfer to any other car. (Impersonal vehicles, of course, stop at many stations along the way, and often require transfers.)

The system should be "user friendly". The passenger will not have to be alert and watch where to get off, as he would with an impersonal system. He should not be required to know anything about various routes or which vehicle to board, or which track to find. A passenger should never have to let several vehicles go by, as with buses or trains, while he waits for and recognizes the proper one.

The passenger should not wait for the vehicle; the vehicle should wait for the passenger. In other words, when the passenger comes to any station of this new technology, the vehicle should be ready for him. If he has to wait at all, it should not be more than a minute or two.

Passengers should never have to stand; a seat should always be available.

People in wheelchairs should be readily accommodated.

Being personal transportation, the system should convey only each individual passenger or one or two additional family members or friends.

Security from assault or robbery would be of prime importance.

Cost of using the service should be similar to rates in effect for impersonal transportation.

The safety of the system should be vastly improved over all traditional modes. It should be impossible for a head-on collision to occur. Collisions with any other type of transportation mode, for example at grade crossings, should not be possible.

An accident involving hundreds of people and the potential for many deaths as in the case of a train wreck, or an accident similar to a bus' rolling over and bursting into flame, killing 40 or more people, should not be possible.

The system should be on-demand 24 hours per day, every day of the year.

In the event of a power company's power failure, the system should be able to keep on running.

The system should be far less polluting than all other forms of conventional transportation.

The vehicles should be unobtrusive and quiet in operation.

The system should be much more efficient than any other form of transportation.

The capital costs of the system should be far less, by a

factor of several times, than conventional transportation systems.

The significance to society of such a system are manifold: reduction in pollution, traffic congestion, transportation subsidies, de-
pendence upon the automobile; better land, parking, and street
use; vastly improved safety and personal security; the saving of
petroleum reserves.

It may seem that such a list is fanciful and entertaining, and
that it can have no practical significance in the real world. *Yet,
incredible as it seems, every one of the above criteria is met by the
transportation renaissance technology!*

Chapter 3

From the Ground Up

All Requirements Fulfilled

It is really true that the new transportation renaissance technology fulfills all the requirements listed in the previous chapter, and, in fact, accomplishes in addition several more milestones of achievement. People are so accustomed to the inconveniences which prevail in the existing modes of impersonal transportation, that they find it difficult to accept that all of these can be eliminated—there must be a catch somewhere.

There is no catch. The new technology is a "win-win" development. It will take its place as one of the truly great inventions of the twentieth century, for, as we enter the twenty-first, *all* the requirements for its successful introduction are completely developed. It will rival the explosion of the Internet phenomenon in its magnitude. By the middle of the twenty-first century, many cities of the world will have it.

As one might imagine, this level of achievement did not happen overnight. Over most of the last half of the 20th century many capable and talented firms and individuals have contributed to the accumulation of the vast body of knowledge we now have. In most of the advanced countries of the world, altogether, billions of dollars have been spent to attain the realization of this dream. We now stand at the threshold of this historic achievement.

The name which has come to be associated with this remarkable

23

development, which has been in nearly universal use for at least the last two dozen years, is Personal Rapid Transit (PRT). Personal Rapid Transit may be defined as a system of public transportation utilizing small (three person) vehicles, running on an elevated guideway, under complete computer control (no drivers), providing nonstop conveyance to destination, in heated or air-conditioned comfort, with a very high degree of safety.

Major Players

It is felt that it might be useful to introduce some of the major players on the PRT scene, to whom later reference may be had. None of these individuals are inventors in the sense of designing operating hardware for systems, as those described later in this chapter, but all have had a hand in shaping the destiny of PRT.

A. Scheffer Lang is an avid promoter of PRT, and serves as Chairman of the Board of Taxi 2000 Corporation, one of the major PRT companies. His work with that company has been exemplary. For this book he has graciously provided a description of the disparity of track gauges of U. S. railroads, in a later chapter on the need for standardization.

Professor Jerry Schneider, now retired from the University of Washington, has had a long involvement with PRT. Apart from his early espousal of PRT concept, he has had a critical role in helping to clarify thinking all over the world both on what PRT is and what it is not. From his long-time post as an engineering professor at the University of Washington, he has tried to help people worldwide to understand the cost and service implications of the various transit modes. Then, over the past 10 years, he carved out a role as the manager of the best worldwide Internet clearinghouse on advanced transit technologies and current developments about them. His service as a board member and vice president of ATRA, the Advanced Transit Association, just ended in January, 2000.

Dr. Jack Irving is recognized for his distinguished work with the Aerospace Corporation, and for publication of one of the first texts on the technical aspects of PRT. His work is discussed later in this chapter.

Catherine G. Burke is the author of *Innovation and Public Policy*, an incisive book which delineates the inability of government to come to grips effectively with a radically new concept such as PRT.

There are three individuals whose work is so extensive that each is treated in a separate chapter. These are: Ray MacDonald, a superb transportation engineer; Dr. Jerold Kieffer, a political scientist who has served his country in distinguished roles and has worked at the top levels of ATRA, the Advanced Transit Association; and Dr. J. Edward Anderson, who is almost universally regarded worldwide as the foremost authority on PRT.

Professor Charles W. Harris is a professor at the graduate school of Harvard University. He is an untiring champion of PRT. His first introduction to PRT came in 1988 when Dr. Anderson joined the faculty of Boston University. Harris asked him to give a presentation on PRT to his study course on land use development. In a letter to the author, Harris relates that Anderson's presentation was so clear and the ideas he shared were so exciting that he was asked to continue these lectures during his whole tenure. Harris further worked with Anderson and his students in classwork and professionally in proposals for specific projects. He also jointly taught a class with Anderson on the "Basics of PRT Systems" as it relates to system and transportation engineering and land use planning, design and development.

Despite all the money that has been spent and the publicity which has been secured to date, the average person does not know what the term "PRT" stands for, and does not know that a transportation renaissance of historic proportions is about to engulf our civilization. One of the purposes of this book is to help to dispel this ignorance.

One organization which has done a great deal to help dispel

such ignorance is *Citizens for PRT* (CPRT), a non-profit Minneapolis-based organization which is now in the process of expanding by establishing new chapters in other interested cities. CPRT and ATRA are easily the two most important non-profit organizations involved with dissemination of information about PRT. In 1999 and 2000, CPRT was very effective in providing the legislature of the state of Minnesota with information regarding PRT, leading to the introduction of legislation regarding funding of PRT. There are hopeful signs that such legislation may become law in the relatively near future; the momentum is building. CPRT regards its role as also contacting other decision makers, such as public officials at every level, and the media. They have also produced an excellent video, in which the role of PRT is simulated with remarkable clarity. They have created a PRT plan for downtown Minneapolis. They have fearlessly confronted special interests, who support other forms of transportation, with the facts in their newsletter, Web page, and in countless forums and meetings. They have done much to expose the light rail installation for Minneapolis as the ineffective, expensive alternative which it is. CPRT is to be commended for doing an excellent job.

A Little History

In order to comprehend the magnitude of the concept of PRT and to gain a background with which to better understand it, documentation of the work of some of the early experimenters and inventors may prove useful and interesting. It is literally true that the concept went "from the ground up". Some of the earliest ideas were conceived as ground-level concepts, but the many advantages of an elevated system soon became apparent. Among these is the fact that grade-crossing accidents cannot then occur as with any other form of transportation. But more than that, the fact that a minimum amount of land need be dedicated became paramount;

in fact, perhaps no land at all, only the right of easement, or "air rights" might be needed.

One of the earliest designs, however, was not at ground level but was suspended. Edward O. Haltom, in the early 1950's in Dallas, Texas was faced with the task of designing a guideway for a proposed monorail system.

Monorails suffer the same disadvantages as railroads. Since the stations are all on the main line, the spacing or time between vehicles must be very large in order to allow time for stopping at the stations. This means that the cars need to be grouped into trains, and that a large, expensive, and visually obtrusive guideway is required to support them.

Haltom may have been the first inventor to discern that many small cars rather than a larger car offered substantial advantages. His design, which he called Monocab, consisted of six-passenger cars suspended from an overhead guideway.

With clear PRT foresight, he envisioned also that the stations would have to be off the main line, and this required the design of a reliable switch. At first he designed a switch which required the movement of the entire guideway. This was too cumbersome to be practical, and he improved his design substantially by providing a second set of wheels which would carry the weight of the cars while negotiating the critical switch section. Although this improvement was still complicated, his concepts were of value, and he finally sold his ideas to a Garland, Texas. firm called Vero, Inc.

Vero improved on Haltom's design substantially, and even built a full-size operating test track. They later sold Monocab to the Rohr Corporation in 1971. The engineers at Rohr further improved the design, and developed a version which was demonstrated at Transpo 72 at Dulles Airport and in 1973 was selected for installation in Las Vegas. Like so many others, fate was not to allow this to come to fruition.

The demise of the Las Vegas installation, along with several others, is admirably detailed in Catherine G. Burke's scholarly work, *Innovation and Public Policy.* If the reader had any lingering questions as to the negative effects of government involvement, they are effectively dispelled upon reading her book. The sub-title of the book is *The Case of PRT*. It is one of the most comprehensive on the subject of PRT and its failure to be implemented. Drawing on countless interviews and public documents, Burke dispassionately details the sordid involvement of government agencies as well as private vested interests. The frailties of human nature and their organizations are exposed for all to see. She extracts conclusions from all of these examples of failed attempts, which are hardly an endorsement of our system of government agencies. For example, she states that UMTA, the Urban Mass Transportation Administration, has done more to discourage than encourage innovative systems.

The Las Vegas case is so fraught with innuendo, overlapping authorities, calls for ever more studies, conflicting and competing agencies and vested interests, greed, envy, distrust and nearly every other human failing that it is impossible to summarize it adequately. Yet the question as to the readiness of the Rohr system for actual introduction was scarcely touched upon, nor was any investigation done on possibly expanding the system into other areas of the community. An interested reader is referred to Burke's extensive coverage.

After the failure at Las Vegas, however, the engineers at Rohr became enamored with another new idea: magnetic suspension of the vehicles. They went on to incorporate this radical concept into their design. And they had another radical concept—linear induction motors for propulsion.

The concept of linear induction motors was a giant step forward in propulsion of vehicles. It is a fascinating development, which has a great many advantages over conventional designs, an important one being that there are no moving parts (other than the moving car). It is perhaps best understood by thinking of it as being constructed by "unrolling" the components of an ordinary induction motor. Thus the stator, or stationary part of a motor, is "unrolled" to form a series of electrical windings which now lie in a long continuous strip, but short enough to be contained in the base of the vehicle. The rotor, which consists of iron bars, is also "unrolled" to form a continuous strip, but one which is continuously duplicated over the entire length of the guideway. The two components operate as close together as practical. Although now in a completely different disposition, the operation is basically the same as in an ordinary induction motor; the windings induce electric currents in the guideway component, which cause magnetic attraction and pulls the vehicle forward. Braking is also accomplished by electro-magnetic forces.

Even though the engineers at Rohr built and tested such a system in Chula Vista, California, the combination of magnetic suspension and linear induction propulsion, which was quite revolutionary, may have been ahead of its time, and was probably the major factor that eventually scuttled the program. However, although not true PRT, Rohr Monocab equipment based on less difficult concepts has found its place in the automatic transit industry in a number of installations.

Another pioneer of major importance, although he did not construct any system, is Donn Fichter, now retired from the New York State Department of Transportation. While a student at Northwestern University, he wrote an article, based on sketches he had made on the margin of the bulletin during a church service. This article, describing his altogether other-worldly transportation system which he called "Veyar", was published in 1957 in the *Northwestern Engineer*. At that time, it probably would not have been published anywhere but in a university paper. Nevertheless, it was truly revolutionary. Fichter had completely grasped the concept of small, fully automated vehicles operating on an elevated guideway, taking passengers to the destination of their choice, whether that might be office buildings, shopping centers, or work places.

He refined his ideas and published a book in 1964 entitled *Individualized Automatic Transit and the City*, which is still in demand; in fact, he happily sold some at the International Conference on PRT & Other Emerging Transportation Systems in

Minneapolis in 1996. His book was a total systems concept, including not only a hardware system but a system integrated into a city. He was one of the first to recognize and stress the necessity for the smallest and lightest-weight cars and hence the smallest and lightest weight guideways possible. Fichter has been honored a number of times, most recently at this conference, where a plaque was awarded him for the first definitive book on PRT. In 1968 he produced a paper which was published in the influential *Highway Research Record.* "They had qualms about accepting it," Fichter is reputed to have said. "They weren't sure they wanted to be associated with such a nutty idea." Fichter was not only one of the first to grasp and publish the fundamental ideas of PRT, but also one of the first to learn that the implementation of PRT requires an unbelievable amount of research, patience, time, and money. But he has not become discouraged. He is still active in PRT circles and serves on the Board of the Advanced Transit Association.

Media attention to PRT has been sporadic, and often detrimental. In contrast, the July 1969 issue of *Scientific American* carried a comprehensive article in which most of the important features of true PRT were recognized and discussed. However, in a complete turnabout, in the October, 1997 special issue of *Scientific American* devoted entirely to forward-looking transportation systems, PRT was not even mentioned, and some systems to which space was devoted were so impractical as to be embarrassing. Letters to the editor from PRT authorities failed to produce any admission of fault. Apparently the editors feel that if PRT has still not been implemented since 1969, it never will be.

As has often been the case in recent developments, single inventors working alone often do not have the ability and the time to produce meaningful results; they are replaced with teams of people comprised of members with disparate skills. A group such as this at the General Motors Research Laboratories were working on an invention called a ground-effects machine in the late 1950's. This was one of the early on-the-ground developments, and did not anticipate the advantages of an elevated system. It was an air-suspended vehicle which could run on a paved road or on various other surfaces. As the machine had no wheels, the application of the linear induction motor to vehicle propulsion was proposed. The electric coils of the motor were on board the vehicles and reacted with conducting plates in the running surface.

To avoid conflict with antitrust laws, a new company, Transportation Technology, Inc., was formed, which in 1971 became a subsidiary of Otis Elevator. A test track was built and the concept tested, and then an actual system was installed and is still in use at Duke University. The air suspension concept, which they called Hovair, had serious drawbacks for automatic transit use, not the least of which was that its U-shaped guideway was a marvelous snow catcher. But this invention deserves credit for one of the early uses of linear induction motors for propulsion in PRT vehicles.

There were many other early pioneers, most of them arriving independently at all the key ideas of personal rapid transit. One of these was Lloyd Berggren who in 1961 conceived the idea of suspending and propelling the vehicle by means of air jets, and demonstrated that it was possible to do so. The shortcoming of his system, which he called Uniflo, was that the noise generated by the air jets required that the vehicles had to be run in an enclosed tube, which was found to be prohibitively costly, especially if glass was used to allow the passengers to see out. His idea eventually went the way of all other attempts at personal rapid transit.

No doubt the best work in this country in the early days was done by The Aerospace Corporation. This was a not-for-profit corporation established by the Air Force to manage its ballistic missile program. In 1967 its Board of Directors determined that some of its talent should be devoted to solving urban problems. A group in The Aerospace Corporation managed by Dr. Jack Irving decided to concentrate on transportation problems. Since they were newcomers to the field, they were not captive to any set of established ideas, and were able to come up with a revolutionary innovation. All of the major concepts of true PRT design were arrived at independently. A one-tenth scale model of their PRT system was built which conclusively proved that PRT was technically feasible. The work done by The Aerospace Corporation still stands as a testament to good engineering and provides the basics for PRT design.

Jack Irving was the spark plug of the organization. He had a PH.D. in Theoretical Physics, having studied at Cal Tech and Princeton. He was a vice president of The Aerospace Corporation since its beginning in 1960 and he had had many years of experience in directing the planning of complex military, space, and information systems and in the area of automatic control. His keen mind grasped the implications of PRT at the outset, and he has remained a committed devotee to the concept.

In November of 1971, as described later, the first International Conference on PRT was held. Jack Irving and his team were present and gave some key presentations. In December 1971 Dr. Larry Goldmuntz of the Office of Science and Technology in the Executive Office of the President invited Jack Irving and J. Edward Anderson to give presentations to the President's Science Advisory Council, which resulted in the inclusion of PRT as the leading new technology initiative in President Nixon's State of the Union Message to Congress in January 1972.

Jack Irving also served on the committees for the 1973 and 1975 PRT Conferences. He and his colleagues have written a book, *Fundamentals of PRT*, one of the few books on the subject.

As a government organization, however, the Aerospace Corporation had no ability to commercialize the work it had done, and could only refer it to others. Its attempts to work with the various bureaucrats at UMTA, the Urban Mass Transportation Administration, at first seemed promising. In 1969 Irving met with Bill Merritt, who was acting associate administrator for research and development at UMTA, and who seemed supportive. But Merritt soon after was made assistant to the newly appointed associate administrator for research and development, Dr. Robert Hemmes. The Aerospace people found it impossible to get an appointment with either Hemmes or Carlos Villareal, the newly appointed administrator of UMTA, so their efforts came to naught. Later on, the Aerospace Corporation became involved with NASA. It's a long story, but this involvement was perceived as a threat by the people at UMTA and dealt with accordingly. Eventually, as has happened so often, the efforts of the Aerospace Corporation received a crippling blow at the hands of conventional transit interests by political opposition in the mid-1970's.

Jerry Kieffer has provided some additional personal details about the workings of UMTA:

> In late 1972, UMTA was being pressured to institute a PRT program. In her wonderful book, Catie Burke traces all the 1972 actions. By January or February, 1973, a memorandum of understanding was submitted for the expected friendly approval of James Beggs, Under Secretary of Transportation, that would seal an agreement between USDOT and the National Aeronautics and Space Administration (NASA) to collaborate on the PRT program, using a NASA team from its missile activities being downsized at Huntsville, Alabama. A fellow by the name of Chuck Elms was head of the team. Elms and team were very enthusiastic about what they considered their certain assignment to build, test and operate this new form of transit.
>
> One day, expecting Beggs approval of the memorandum of understanding that afternoon, they met at my house with wine bottles, ready for use the minute they got a call indicating that Beggs had signed the agreement. After some hours, nothing happened. Nor did anything happen the next day and so on, except that right then the Nixon White House eased Beggs out of office. All presidential appointees (including me, as Assistant Administrator of the foreign aid agency) had to submit resignations to the president after Nixon's reelection in November, 1972. I was asked to stay. It turned out that the Secretary of Transportation, John Volpe

and Under Secretary Beggs were thanked and let go. Indeed, through a back channel I had to the White House, I learned that I was on a short list for persons who might succeed Beggs as Under Secretary. However, no one ever spoke to me about such an appointment. (Consider what might have been the future of PRT had I been appointed!) Anyway, a White House staffer by the name of Egil Krogh was tapped for the job, but he lasted only a few months, because it was uncovered that he had been one of the so-called "White House plumbers" involved in the Watergate scandal. Neither he nor his successor focused on PRT, and the project's life was ended.

There were serious attempts at PRT in both England and France. In the late 1960's the Royal Aircraft Establishment was commissioned by the British Government to study the PRT concept. The inventor, Dr. Leslie R. Blake, who named the system Cabtrack, had come to the United States to look at the Alden StaRRcar system (described later), the Urbmobile and other systems. Substantial progress was made, even to the extent that a one-fifth scale model test track was built. A contract was even awarded for the integration into a city. But it failed, as so many efforts have, because of a quirk of human nature. In the 1972 elections, a new Minister of Environment was appointed. He had never heard of the PRT initiative, and no one briefed him about it. He was deeply insulted when the first he knew about it was from reading the newspaper. He refused to authorize the program or any further funding.

Work on the the French "Aramis" PRT system was begun in 1969 and reached the test track level of development, but was never really a viable system. While it was true PRT and utilized four-passenger cars, it was saddled with many faults. However, a prototype test track of one kilometer was built at Orly Airport in Paris in 1973, and tests were carried out for a number of years. The great contribution of the French effort was to demonstrate that headways as short as .2 seconds—roughly 12 inches between vehicles—were feasible. But the French, like their counterparts in the other countries, were up against the entrenched forms of transportation. It is said that millions of francs were spent before the developmental authorities finally realized the hopelessness of the situation and killed the program in 1987.

It is interesting that some of the biggest names in American industry have at various times been actively associated with the PRT concept. These include General Motors (ground effects machine), Otis Elevator (Hovair), Raytheon (PRT 2000), and the Ford Motor Company and Westinghouse. Ford developed an impractical 24 passenger vehicle for which there was no market. Westinghouse opposed PRT because of their own development of their large-vehicle on-line-station automatic system which has found its niche as an automatic people-mover in a number of airports.

It is estimated by some sources that the incredible sum of over two billion dollars has been spent worldwide on all aspects of PRT by all the companies and governments which have been involved since its inception. All of this, however, was not a tragic waste of manpower and resources. Quite a bit of it helped to produce the body of knowledge we now possess which positions PRT on the very edge of fulfillment.

Chapter 4

Successful Testings

The Surprising Maturity of the Technology

It may come as a surprise to realize that the degree of PRT maturity is much greater than is conventionally recognized. When it is compared with other inventions, or particularly with other inventions relating to transportation, this fact comes to light.

Thus, for example, PRT is much farther evolved than the science of aviation was after the Wright brothers had completed their historic flight. That was the first successful American test of manned flight. PRT has already had many successful testings.

In fact, the aviation industry continued for quite some time simply to demonstrate and improve on the technique of airborne flight, without yet beginning to concentrate on and develop the specifics of air transportation. The emphasis was on exploiting the novelty, and, in the early days before the advent of the airliners, one could purchase a ticket to go on a flight for the fun of it on one of the early planes, such as the Ford Tri-motor.

In contrast, the novelty of PRT, while real enough, is secondary; the primary purpose from its inception always had been to provide improved public transportation. As early as thirty years ago it would have been possible to build and install a true PRT system, had the desire been strong enough. Such a system, however, would have been rather quaint by today's standards, given the technology we now have at our disposal. It is perhaps advantageous that actual installation has not occurred until the present. We now have the modern PRT design, which embodies every desirable feature to carry us well into the twenty-first century without change.

It may seem quite a conundrum that even though a number of the early systems were actually tested and successfully demonstrated with full size test tracks and cars, they were never actually used. The testing usually revealed some previously unnoticed or disregarded flaw which sufficed to render the concept uneconomical. However, all of these tests contributed to the growing body of knowledge in regard to PRT, in many cases what *not* to do as well as what to do.

Actual Testings

In the case of Haltom's Monocab, Vero, Inc., who purchased his invention, went on to design a much better switch, and built and tested a full-size test track in 1969. However, they were unable to sell the product to anyone interested in actually using it, and they ultimately sold this invention to the Rohr Corporation.

The engineers at Rohr improved on the invention they had received from Vero, Inc. and developed a version, which was demonstrated at Transpo72 at Dulles Airport and in 1973 was selected for installation in Las Vegas, but actual installation never went ahead.

As mentioned previously, the engineers at Rohr thought that the product could be improved by using magnetic suspension along with linear induction propulsion. To build such a system in those days must have been quite a feat, but it was accomplished; Rohr built and tested such a system in Chula Vista, California. However, a difficulty which proved to be insurmountable was that the engineers tried to combine the magnetic suspension properties with the linear propulsion in the same electrical windings. This combination proved to be incompatible, and the program eventually had to be abandoned.

The Transportation Technology, Inc. group with its air suspension machine called Hovair went on to develop a full-scale testing facility in Detroit in 1969. Otis Elevator had one success in marketing the product; their system has been in daily operation at Duke University Medical Center for over twenty years. However, the cost of the wide guideway, the visual impact, and the fact that it is a snow catcher, have precluded any further sales of the Hovair system.

Lloyd Berggren, who used air jets to suspend and propel his vehicle, suffered no better fate than all the others. His system, which he called Uniflo, produced so much noise that it was not practical to run the vehicles in the open air; therefore, he was obliged to enclose the system in a tube. However, Berggren was able to obtain funding from the Rosemount Engineering Company of Minneapolis to build a full-scale test track, but it turned out to be just one more example of a system which was successfully demonstrated, but could never be used. The cost of the enclosure, particularly if glass was used to enable the passengers to see out, was simply too much. Also, it proved necessary to air condition the whole tube, which again was prohibitively expensive.

These examples of the inventions of the early pioneers, each of which, remarkably, was successfully tested, serve to point out just how fraught with danger the path to true PRT installation really is.

There are three further examples which, although they were more practical than any of the above, still were proven by the marketplace not to be viable alternatives. These are treated in the following chapters.

Dr. J. Edward Anderson gives further examples of the efforts of the early experimenters. in his treatise, "Some Early History of PRT", and also in his paper, "Some Lessons from the History of PRT".

It is certainly appropriate to question why, in view of all these nominal successes, PRT has never been actually installed as a real system anywhere in the world. Surely it would seem that somehow,

PRT would have been tried by this time. Catherine Burke sheds considerable light on this subject in her remarkable book, *Innovation and Public Policy*, in which she details how difficult it is for government agencies to make the leap of faith to a revolutionary new technology. Dr. Anderson answers this question quite extensively in his paper, "Why, After Decades, Has Personal Rapid Transit Not Yet Been Widely Accepted?", which he authored in 1997. This paper is reproduced herein as Appendix A.

Chapter 5

Cabintaxi

The Invention

The Cabintaxi story is one of the most fascinating of the PRT developments. It was developed in Germany when interest in the new idea was running high in many quarters. At the time the invention was in full swing, there was every expectation that the system would be a resounding success. The German government was solidly behind the effort, providing financial and technical assistance. Cabintaxi was probably the first system to deliver practically all of the advantages of PRT.

The invention was the brainchild of Dr. Klaus Becker, who, with typical German ingenuity and persistence, had guided the invention to its complete maturity. There is no question but that Dr. Becker's work contributed a great deal to the evolution of PRT. With characteristic thoroughness, the German designers submitted the program to extensive analysis of the various alternatives for suspension, switching, motor design, cabin size and track size, ultimately settling upon a system of three-passenger cabs. They were ahead of others in perceiving the advantages of linear induction motors.

Becker's invention did not suffer from many of the common faults of the systems of previous inventors. He did not use air or magnetic levitation for suspension; he did not need to enclose the system in a tube; and, although a large amount of snow could still

41

pose somewhat of a problem, he did not use a large, U-shaped trough as a guideway, a natural snow catcher, as others had. He recognized that small, lightweight cars and a corresponding lightweight guideway were two elements crucial to the success of a PRT system.

The Cabintaxi system was received with great fanfare in Germany. A full-size prototype was built on which people could ride, which clearly demonstrated all of the advantages of PRT. Actual testing began in 1973 and was carried to successful completion. Following this, a large variety of tests were undertaken concerning reliability, maintenance, and the human factors, in preparation for offering the system for actual use. An ambitious planning program was undertaken to study the installation in various German cities. The demonstration layout consisted of a large number of cars, together with a full size station for boarding. It almost could have served as a small installation, such as a park facility. Excellent movies of the system in operation were produced, showing people entering and exiting the cars and showing the cars in operation. These movies are still being used to demonstrate the principles of PRT. The boxy appearance of the cars, looking rather like oversize telephone booths moving stiffly around the track, left something to be desired. Aerodynamic design apparently was not felt necessary, given the low speeds of operation.

The design was greatly complicated in that it involved cars running above the guideway, and also cars running below the guideway and suspended from it. This may have been to demonstrate that Cabintaxi was functional in either concept, the clear superiority of the cars above the guideway not having as yet emerged in PRT concept. The design of cars running below could have been eliminated, leaving a very viable system.

The German invention of Cabintaxi was highly influenced by a series of reports, which were made public, under a study undertaken by the Housing and Urban Development (HUD) of the United States. It is interesting that the tax dollars of U.S. citizens helped to promote the development of this German system.

The Passing

The demise of the Cabintaxi system in Germany came, as it has so many times in the United States, at the hands of the railroad die-hards, who perceived PRT as a threat to their continued dominance, to be discredited at any cost. The story has it than one of the railroad officials, in searching for means to stop PRT, discovered an old law which mandated that bridge plates for railroad work were required to be twelve millimeters thick. Somehow he got the courts to agree that this law would include any type of public conveyance operating on rails or a guideway. This included PRT even though the cars were a small fraction of the weight of a railroad car. Since all of the structure was elevated, it was all considered to be under the category of bridges, and, therefore, the entire supporting structure of the guideway had to be made of steel twelve millimeters thick, instead of the eight millimeters which Becker had planned. He was faced with a terrible dilemma: either they had to go along, or fight the court system and the railroads. In the end, the Cabintaxi forces capitulated, but it resulted in a guideway design which was grossly over-designed and which could not compete effectively against the entrenched forces.

The coup de grace was delivered by the German government. In 1980 Germany had to come up with a substantial budget for NATO defenses as its contribution. Prime Minister Helmut Schmidt mandated that all unnecessary civilian programs be eliminated. This included all experimental projects like Cabintaxi. Without the government funds needed to proceed, the project abruptly ended. The system has never materialized in actual practice, either here or abroad, but it is still represented in the U. S. by Mr. Marsden Burger, who is being paid to market the product. It is certainly conceivable that Cabintaxi or a revision thereof may still become one of the prominent players on the PRT scene, particularly after the viability of PRT has been proved in actual development and usage.

However, much work would be needed before this could occur. Mr. Burger testified before a committee of ATRA, The Advanced Transportation Association, an organization conceived and commissioned at one of the International Conferences on PRT described in a later chapter. (ATRA's mission is to further the development of new or improvements in existing forms of transportation. In 1989, ATRA produced its landmark study of PRT.) Mr. Burger testified before the technical committee for this study, conceding that the two German companies that own Cabintaxi had no project budget and no project team in existence. The "project" he said at that point was simply himself and a bunch of files. He also stated that Cabintaxi would have to license someone else's control system and probably other components before it could become viable.

The Shortcomings

Although the Cabintaxi design was among the first to recognize most of the valuable attributes of PRT, its design was not without serious faults. One of these was its attempt to incorporate the use of vehicles both above and below the guideway. The concept of cars suspended from a guideway inherently makes the design of the supporting posts much more difficult and expensive; they would have to be built more strongly in order to bear the off-center load, and would have to be at one side of the guideway. However, the most serious fault with all suspended designs is in connection with the switching.

In car-above-guideway designs, it is simple to make the running surfaces for the wheels continuous for both divergences of the track. In order to do this, the wheels cannot have flanges as in railroad practice; they have cushioned rubber tires. Thus the vehicle can go either way, and which way it goes can be determined by other means than physical movement of the track elements. This is the governing precept of the on-board switch, which is fundamental to modern PRT design and is fully described in a later chapter.

In car-below-guideway designs, this simplicity does not hold. Since the structure to hang the car must extend downward from the wheels, a little thought will disclose that this structure, whether interior or exterior to the track, must somehow cut across the running surfaces when switching. The running surfaces therefore cannot be continuous as in the car-above-guideway designs. Thus the suspended systems have all had to contend with this problem; the solution usually being that some part of the track system must move. An alternate solution is to unload the main support wheels during switching by means of other wheels expressly for this purpose, which makes a complicated design. Either way, the simplicity and safety of the above-guideway system are lost.

Cabintaxi, however, could have eliminated the suspended element completely and thereby had a viable system, but there is no evidence that they intended to do so. This would mean giving up the concept of operation in both directions from a single guideway, which is inherent in the Cabintaxi design.

U. S. Marketing Attempts

One of the early proponents of personal rapid transit already alluded to was Dr. J. Edward Anderson. It was early in his career in PRT. He had yet to recognize the pivotal role he would ultimately play in the eventual commercialization of PRT. In 1973 when Cabintaxi was first demonstrated, he saw himself only as one who might make some measurable contribution to its success.

His growing stature among his contemporaries was already

recognizable. He had earlier written many papers and lectured abroad. On one of his many trips abroad, Anderson met Dr. Klaus Becker, the inventor and promoter of the Cabintaxi system, whom Anderson called a genius. (Dr. Becker later was a member of ATRA's Board of Directors.) Thus Anderson's name came to the attention of the German owners of the Cabintaxi system. At the time, the system was up against formidable opposition by the railroad systems in Germany, and the company thought that they might be able to market their system abroad, particularly in the United States. In 1977 they approached Ed Anderson, questioning whether he might represent them in selling the system, and also in finding an American manufacturer who would be willing to take on the line and manufacture the system for the U. S. market.

At the time, this seemed like a golden opportunity to Ed Anderson. There was no viable U. S. system which even approached Cabintaxi in its degree of sophistication. This would be a way to get PRT up and running in this country. Other manufacturing entities would be sure to follow. Anderson devoted his full energies to this end.

The story of his efforts to market the Cabintaxi system is related in the chapter entitled "With the Help of a Pro". He was one of many who were initially disappointed by the failure to achieve success with Cabintaxi, but later came to realize what a blessing in disguise it really was; it left him free to become ultimately the world's foremost authority on personal rapid transit.

Chapter 6

Morgantown

The Original Inventor

The Morgantown advanced transportation system is an example of what can happen when government forces take charge of a project.

William Alden was one of the early experimenters who contributed much to the advancement of PRT, and who unfortunately has not received the credit which is his due. He was a gifted inventor who was able to grasp the possibilities of PRT well in advance of the conventional knowledge of his time. His early ideas embraced the so-called "dual mode" concept, in which it was conceived that vehicles could be built which could be driven on the streets and highways like an automobile, but which would embody the technology to enable them to enter a ramp to a guideway, then operate on the guideway under fully automatic control. Bill Alden called this design StaRRcar (Self-Transit Rail and Road car). It wasn't too long until Bill Alden realized the shortcomings of dual mode and began to concentrate instead on regular or single mode PRT.

In a very innovative move, Alden and the associates of his company designed and built a one-twentieth scale model replica of his system. With this system they were able to demonstrate conclusively that short headway distances were not only possible but also practical and safe. Rather than being expressed in distance, headway is usually stated in terms of the number of seconds between

47

cars passing a given point. This measure takes into account both the velocity of the cars and their separation distance, and is more meaningful to PRT designers. With their model system, Alden and his group were able to definitely show that headways as short as 1.6 seconds were practical.

The author is indebted to Bob Fillmore, an engineer who joined Alden on May 1, 1971, and worked on the Morgantown project. He has graciously provided many of the particulars of the story of Morgantown. He relates that Alden's company designed and built at Bedford, Maine an oval test track, with two stations and several cars. At Bedford, Bob Fillmore, working with Alden, was able to demonstrate speed control and origin-to-destination travel. The vehicle was propelled by a hydrostatic pump and hydraulic motors geared to the wheels. This drive was commonly used on mobile equipment such as bituminous pavers and motor graders at this time. The hydraulic motor propulsion worked well enough, but was not so efficient and reliable as linear induction motors which other experimenters had been using.

The vehicle seated six persons on two facing bench seats. It was not commonly realized at the time that six person capacity not only results in excessive vehicle weight and poor passenger distribution (PRT ridership is expected to average about 1.1 persons per car), but it also invites car sharing and loses the safety advantage of not having to ride with strangers.

Alden made one great contribution, somehow divining that the on-board switch would greatly improve safety and allow much closer headways (distance between cars) than had been previously possible. By means of his on-board switch, the car was guided to remain on the main line by the left rail, and was guided into the stations by the right rail (no moving parts in the track). Although Alden's on-board switch was crude by today's standards, it remains as his enduring legacy. The refined standards of present PRT technology could not exist without this milestone contribution.

The vagaries of fortune and history are what makes fascinating reading about nearly any major invention. What happened to Bill

Alden's invention could not have been imagined by him in his wildest speculations.

The story is told of Leo Bakeland, the inventor of the patented process for developing and printing photographs, which he called Velox. The development of the box camera, the snapshot, in fact the whole field of personal and amateur photography had been hindered by the lack of a good process. George Eastman of Eastman Kodak was very much aware of the potential in this field, and became appraised of Bakeland's invention. He gave him a call.

"I'd like you to come up to Boston," he told Bakeland. "We're interested in your invention. I think we can come to terms."

Riding up in the train, Bakeland debated with himself whether to ask $25,000, which was a lot of money in those days. He had still not answered this question in his mind when he arrived.

George Eastman cordially ushered him into his office. After some preliminary discussion, he said, "We've decided to offer you one million dollars for your invention. Will that be satisfactory?"

Bakeland somehow managed to retain his composure, and accepted.

With a small part of the money, Bakeland first took a wonderful trip abroad with his family. He then settled down to resuming his life work in chemical engineering and designing. Ultimately he produced a strong, rugged plastic compound which he foretold would have a multitude of uses. He called it "Bakelite".

Political Influences

In the case of William Alden, fate did not deal so kindly. At the time of his invention, the U. S. Government, in its bumbling way, had some perception that there possibly might be something to this new concept of transportation. At the same time, unbeknownst to Alden, Professor Samy Elias, head of the Industrial

Engineering Department of the University of West Virginia, was
concerned over the traffic problems in Morgantown, particularly
in relation to his alma mater. Morgantown is built in a narrow
river gorge, and all the traffic from one end to the other funnels
through this constriction. This particularly affected the university's
three campuses, which are separated by some little distance. With
the help of the legislature of West Virginia and others, Elias was
able to convince UMTA, the Urban Mass Transportation
Administration, to designate $50,000 toward the study of
comparable PRT systems as being possible solutions to the
problem.

Bill Alden's StaRRcar was no longer dual mode, and was the
foremost U.S. development at the time. His system was selected in
1970 as best system available. (Actually, it was the only practical one of the three systems studied.) In the study and proposal
to the University of West Virginia, Alden engineers had proposed
stations, guideways, power pickups, and steering. Patents had been
applied for in all of these areas.

From this point onward, we see unfolding how the heavy hand
of government ruined a potential PRT application. The University
of West Virginia accepted the Alden proposal and went to the
state and federal government for funding.

A follow-on proposal was made, which the Department of
Transportation took seriously, to go into the engineering of the
system. At that time conventional wisdom had it that only two
years would be required to complete a successful PRT system. John
A. Volpe, the Secretary of Transportation, became interested when
it was realized that it might be possible to make political hay from
such a project. Catherine Burke, author of *Innovation and Public
Policy*, points out that there was a whole galaxy of political power
in Washington at the time with ties to the University of West
Virginia, and Volpe was an astute politician. If the project could
be completed in time for Richard Nixon to ride on it, coincidental
with his second run for the Presidency, the administration could
be shown to be a great advocate of progress and new ideas. In fact,

Nixon passed the word that he wanted to go into the elections of 1972 as a backer of innovative science and technology projects that would give him a very progressive image. Moreover, as he was confident of being re-elected in 1972, he assumed that he would be the nation's sitting president in 1976, when America's bicentennial would be celebrated. Therefore, he wanted to be able to showcase projects brought to reality by that time.

Robert Byrd, the Democratic senator from West Virginia, also became a supporter, as one would expect from his record of bringing home the pork. Senator Jennings Randolph, Democrat, West Virginia (now deceased), was also influential in getting the Morgantown project on its way.

In 1971, Larry Goldmuntz, who later became Chair of ATRA, the Advanced Transit Association, served on the staff of Nixon's Office of Science and Technology. He was instrumental in placing in Nixon's planned State of the Union message for January, 1972, a strong plug for a new mode of urban transit that, as described, really was PRT. Lead stories were given out to the press about this project initiative along with other ideas. However, something unexplained happened before the message was delivered to the Congress. As delivered, the PRT-like project was never mentioned by Nixon. The message was silent on new forms of transit. Someone in the White House staff got cold feet and took the reference out. Goldmuntz was so angry that not long after he resigned from his job and left the government.

UMTA, in its infinite wisdom, decided that Bill Alden's small company was no match for the job of completing the project within the approximate two-year period. While this was probably true, the folly was to mandate completion of an untried technology within such a short time frame, or *any* time frame.

The Jet Propulsion Laboratory, a NASA facility, was chosen to be systems manager. Bob Fillmore recalls that he was told that officials of the Jet Propulsion Laboratory came to Bedford and met with Bill Alden and his staff. They made it clear that the system would be a JPL system and not the Alden system. The requests for bids requiring engineering, quality control and manufacturing capabilities went far beyond Alden's ability to fill.

But Alden at least had a hand in procuring the new players. Alden sought out Raytheon to be the vehicle manufacturer, which declined; but in a bold move right from their offices, Alden called Boeing, which accepted. Boeing and Alden made an agreement to bid for the vehicles and the controls. The F. R. Harris Engineering Company was selected by JPL for the design and construction of the guideway. The control system was awarded to the Bendix Company. Boeing and Alden were awarded the vehicle contract, but, beyond that association, Bill Alden had no control over what happened to his fledgling PRT system.

President Nixon was in favor of the efforts of Secretary Volpe and Senator Byrd, and even made a speech in which he said that the same people (The Jet Propulsion Laboratory) that took three men 250,000 miles in space to walk on the moon were now going to take 250,000 people three miles across town.

The Debacle

The whole development was a fiasco, almost from the beginning. With such an imminent deadline breathing down their necks, the huge corporations involved had almost no time for the patient testing, conferences between participants, and the usual modeling procedures which are a normal part of any such new, large-scale development. All rushed pell-mell to get their portion of the contracts completed in time. Harris Engineering, having no knowledge of the weight and characteristics of the vehicles being developed by Boeing, proceeded to develop a guideway which was far overdesigned, a huge construction of no esthetic quality. Boeing, for its part, was proceeding well with its designs when the heavy hand of UMTA again interfered. UMTA arbitrarily decided that the 1.6 second headways conclusively demonstrated by Bill Alden with his model system were unsafe, and could not be relied upon in a real system. Bendix, having had no experience with true PRT, bid a block system of control requiring 15 second headway. This seemed reasonable to UMTA, which therefore declared a headway time of 15 seconds.

The chaos which this introduced is hard to imagine. Now it was no longer possible to convey the anticipated ridership in Alden's six passenger cars, arriving 1.6 seconds apart. Boeing was obliged to design much larger cars, carrying eight persons seated and twelve standing, in order to accommodate the expected ridership in peak periods. Out the window went one of the basic principles of PRT design, small cars. Any remote resemblance to Bill Alden's StaRRcar had vanished. Although UMTA later reduced the headway to 7.5 seconds, still far too long, the damage had been done.

In the supreme irony, it turned out that Bendix had underbid Boeing and Alden by more than one million dollars for the control system and thus was awarded the contract, even though it did not meet the requirements for short headways. No one noticed that the Bendix bid did not include manuals, but the Boeing and Alden bid did. It cost over one million dollars to get Bendix to supply the manuals.

The larger cars introduced a new problem. The curves on the guideway built by Harris Engineering were not designed for such large cars; it was found that they could not negotiate the curves. To redesign the guideway at this late stage was impossible; some of it was already erected. Boeing had to go back to the drawing board and redesign the cars to provide for both front and back wheel steering to make the curves.

Sometime during the design of the guideway process it occurred to someone to check whether it ever snows in Morgantown. They found that it does. In fact, it snows quite a bit. The U-shaped design of the guideway was a perfect snow catcher. It was impossible to plow this, because of the interruption of service and because of the delicate and dangerous power rails and other details within the guideway. The only remaining alternative was to melt the snow by embedding in the guideway pipes carrying heated ethylene glycol. A former University of Minnesota student who worked on the project showed that the cost necessary to melt the snow would be over four times that required to operate the vehicles.

The effect which these events had upon the projected costs was predictable: they soared out of sight. Morgantown was lampooned in the press as the boondoggle of the century. Far from being a political asset, the Morgantown transportation system seemed headed for disaster. In late 1971 The Jet Propulsion Laboratory was replaced by Boeing as Systems Manager, and the word came from UMTA that the system must be dedicated before the 1972 election.

Bob Fillmore recalls that, in 1972, production at Bill Alden's company and at Boeing were carried on around the clock. Cost control was not an objective.

Somehow at the final hour, the system, through sheer dogged determination, was rescued. Boeing obviously did not want its reputation impaired by this monstrosity, which, though a small increment of Boeing's balance sheet, threatened to produce a blight of monumental proportions. Pulling together, despite the government intervention and the efforts of the press, the contractors managed to get the system into operation. But President Nixon did not get to make much, if any, political hay from the development. By the time it was completed, the system had received so much bad publicity from the colossal cost overruns and bus-like size of the vehicles, that it was hardly a monument to the foresight of the administration.

Then an event occurred which did not help matters any. In a public relations move, Patricia Nixon was scheduled to dedicate the system and to ride on it in its opening triumph in October, 1972. The dedication ceremony went well enough. There were five cars completed and several stations were operable. But in their zeal to insure reliability, the contractors had fitted the system with numerous fail-safe detectors and switches to ensure the safety of the passengers. The problem was, if one of these operated, the result was to shut down the system until the fault was repaired. Sure enough, one of these devices failed internally (there was nothing wrong on the system) and Tricia Nixon was obliged to sit in the car for quite some time until the fault was discovered. The press, of course, gleefully reported on this event.

The troubles at Morgantown were far from over with the dedication event. Only five of the intended fifteen vehicles were operational, and the problems that developed with these first vehicles were so great that serious consideration was given to junking them. The students said that PRT stood for *pretty rotten transit*. A monumental dispute arose between the University and UMTA. The University wanted a working system and attractive stations, and UMTA was forced to use much of the additional money which was to have been used for research and development on making the system more attractive.

The university had the right in their contract to require removal of the system entirely if it was not satisfactory. They threatened to exercise this right unless things were put right, which required the expenditure of still more money to improve reliability and performance.

PRT Dragged Down with Morgantown

There is no dispute that the cause of PRT was set back immeasurably by the Morgantown debacle. Congress demanded an investigation by the General Accounting Office, and the Senate requested a study by the U.S. Office of Technology Assessment of the whole automated transit area.

The OTA study was a classic case of anti-PRT loading. The people who designed the study deliberately chose the most costly version of PRT (that no responsible PRT person had ever suggested) and then concluded that PRT as a concept was too high cost. It would be the same as choosing to study one of those very high cost foreign autos as a model for autos and then concluding that autos as a travel mode are too high cost.

The media was quick to point out that PRT was far more expensive than forecast, and that it did not run reliably. The sad fact was that they denigrated the whole concept of PRT; the Morgantown installation as finally built no longer represented true PRT in any fashion. The personal attribute of PRT had been compromised by the large cars; it no longer took you individually where you wanted to go. The large headway arbitrarily imposed by UMTA was unacceptable to good PRT design. And the huge guideway, dominating the landscape and proving to be a marvelous snow catcher, was the complete antithesis of the PRT concept.

It literally has taken many years to recover from the shock of Morgantown. Government support for PRT ground to a standstill, from which it has never recovered. The congress canceled funds which had been earmarked for the city of Denver, to construct a test track in the suburb of Broomfield. This effectively dealt the deathblow to the extensive plans Denver had for PRT. Boeing spent some years trying to market the system, but has never found another buyer. And Morgantown came on the heels of another fiasco, the control system failure of the BART development in 1972 on the West Coast which resulted in a serious accident. BART was not PRT at all but was still associated in the mind of the public as being all of the same mold.

In 1974, Dr. Anderson would write: "The scars of the Morgantown project still so strongly affect the research and development activities of the Urban Mass Transportation Administration that it is not at all clear how soon Congress will be willing to authorize another major program to develop PRT systems." His words have turned out to be more prophetic than he probably realized. Since that time, Congress has never authorized any further funds specifically for a PRT project.

And yet, Morgantown did accomplish some noteworthy achievements. Perhaps the most important thing it has demonstrated conclusively is that automatic control is practical. The vehicles on the system operate entirely automatically; there are no drivers or motormen. Another aspect which the system has fully demonstrated is one of safety. For over twenty-seven years, the system at Morgantown has operated automatically without a serious accident of any kind. This is mute testimony to the fact that the judgment of the automatic controllers is far superior to that of human drivers, who are subject to all the frailties of the human condition. These facts are not particularly newsworthy, at least in the estimation of many editors, so they have not been extensively chronicled. We don't read anything about Morgantown anymore; certainly not any of its positive aspects.

The ghosts of Morgantown are still around to haunt us. Every now and then, someone, often a government official, vaguely remembers that PRT was discredited by some system built years ago, which was a comedy of errors and cost four times as much as we were told it would. They don't know that, once the bugs were taken out, the system has continued to run almost flawlessly since Nixon's time, carrying over fifty million passengers in far better style than the best bus or light rail system, and with an unsurpassed safety record.

Chapter 7

Raytheon

The Rapprochement

Of all the systems which have been developed, successfully tested, but never actually installed, the development by Raytheon is probably the most impressive. While it had some monumental faults, it did embody many of the major principles of true PRT. Designated as PRT-2000, it was proposed for the Chicago Regional Transportation Authority, (RTA), and was intended for use by the suburb of Rosemont in providing transportation between major hotels, conferences centers, and businesses, with a direct link the the RTA's existing Blue Line rail system.

Here is another case of what can happen when an excellent design is taken over by a huge enterprise, in this case the Raytheon Corporation rather than the U. S. Government. The story begins with Dr. J. Edward Anderson, who has been at the forefront of PRT research and development for over 30 years. In his early years as a professor at the University of Minnesota, Dr. Anderson's participation was more general than specific; that is, he was more interested in developing and creating a literature base and promoting the cause of PRT generally than he was in any specific design. In 1971, however, he made the deliberate decision not to try to design his own system, but to try to implement the best PRT system then available, which was the German-designed Cabintaxi system. It was after the unavailability of Cabintaxi, together with its perceived shortcomings, that led directly to his beginning work on his own design.

Years later, in May of 1989, when his design had been patented and a corporate entity established, he was able to gain an audience with Gayle Franzen, who was chairman of the Chicago RTA at the time. Anderson had spent his early years as a principal engineer at Honeywell, heading up teams of engineers concentrating on various space flight components which Honeywell was developing. His good friend John David Mooney was a Chicago sculptor who was instrumental in lining up the meeting with Franzen. He told Anderson that Franzen had said, "There must be a rocket scientist out there somewhere with a new design for transportation."

"Do you know who that is?" Mooney asked Anderson.

"well . . ."

"Why, it's you, that's who! You're a former rocket scientist, and you're by far the best informed proponent of PRT!"

So it was arranged. The meeting was also attended by Tom Riley, a Chicago businessman, and Dick Daly from Anderson's company, Taxi 2000 Corporation. Gayle Franzen was skeptical at first, but by the end of the meeting, the Taxi 2000 pair had convinced him of the many advantages and the practicality of PRT.

As a result of this meeting, the RTA initiated a program to design PRT for its needs. Taxi 2000 was the winner of an international competition, sponsored by the RTA, established to produce the most acceptable design for a PRT system.

The role of a study of PRT produced by ATRA, the Advanced Transit Association, was quite important. Anderson says, in fact, that the acceptance of the concept of PRT by the RTA board would not have been possible without the influence of the ATRA study of PRT, begun in 1988, described in detail in the chapter entitled *Advanced Transit Association*. ATRA adopted its PRT assessment report at its January, 1989 meeting. Tom Floyd, then ATRA's chairman, and Jerry Kieffer as co-writers of the report, wrote into it that public officials concerned with urban transportation ought to get themselves briefed on the important findings and conclusions presented in the report. Floyd happened to be a close friend of a fellow who worked at WMATA, the Washington Metrorail organization, and who had gone to work for the Chicago area RTA. Through this person, Floyd was able to get the report into the hands of Gayle Franzen. Franzen later told Kieffer how important that report had been to his thinking.

Time passed. At that first critical meeting, the assumption had been that Taxi 2000 would team up with Raytheon, and that Taxi 2000 would play a lead role in that team. But Gayle Franzen and others who were initially enthusiastic were gone from the scene. As had happened with Bill Alden's company, it became clear that Ed Anderson's small company was not in any position to be the prime contractor. Anderson had been working with Raytheon off and on for many years, and their enthusiasm had run the gamut from support to rejection on several occasions. This time they also initially rejected, but changed their mind at the final hour. Had they not done so, the contract would have gone to Intamin, LTD, another promoter of a PRT system.

The Contractual Squeeze

Raytheon's acceptance was based on a contractual agreement in which they would procure not only Anderson's patents, which had been acquired by the University of Minnesota, but also Anderson's extensive know-how in the field. It was an ironclad contract, the product of Raytheon's aggressive legal department, which extorted the very lifeblood out of Anderson's struggling corporation. But the principals at Taxi 2000 and representatives from the university felt they had no recourse but to agree. After all, the one million dollar compensation was a consideration, and enabled Taxi 2000 to pay off many of the debts it owed to sympathetic individuals who over the years had helped with time and money to bring PRT to its then level of development.

This contract in hand, Raytheon then proceeded to execute a

separate contract with the Chicago RTA, which gave Raytheon wide latitude in design and execution, subject to the input of the RTA. Raytheon and the RTA agreed to commit $20 million each to the development of a testing facility to be built on Raytheon's grounds at Marlborough, Massachusetts. The work went ahead.

Even though Anderson was listed as one of the "key personnel" in the contract, this arrangement effectively barred Taxi 2000 from contributing in a meaningful way to the ongoing development. Raytheon had acquired the rights to patents and know-how, but was not obligated in any way to use either them or Anderson's expertise.

Still, the relationship between Raytheon and Ed Anderson started off well enough. Ed was to conduct a two-week course on PRT to their staff, which he did in two segments in October, 1993. Unfortunately a number of key people were not yet assigned and did not take the course. It later became clear that this had disastrous results.

Not Invented Here

The "not invented here" syndrome is a very common phenomenon, known to practically all engineers who have had occasion to deal with patents and trade secrets between companies. It takes various forms, but in essence it is the attitude that "Our company has the best brains in the business. Since it wasn't invented here, it can't be as good as what we can produce, once we set our minds to it." Ed Anderson, as well as many of his peers, had seen this in operation many times in his career with Honeywell and in PRT. It is such a common phenomenon that some companies find it necessary to set up whole new divisions or subsidiaries with people in charge who are reliable proponents of the technology, and new employees who are indoctrinated with the virtue of the original idea, in order to avoid this propensity of human nature. It has been called the curse of the engineering fraternity.

The engineers who took charge of the PRT development at Raytheon were not immune to this malady. Ed Anderson's early suspicions were confirmed when he was relegated to a "make-work" position with no real input into the design decisions that were being made. But there was nothing he could do. It is important to understand that PRT was a miniscule segment of the Raytheon defense contractor juggernaut. Although Anderson was listed as one of the "key personnel", for him even to get a hearing with the higher-up authorities over these matters was almost impossible, and, if achieved, would have produced probably only a curt reference to the contract which had been executed.

Anderson also had no inroads or proper contact with the RTA authorities. Gayle Franzen and others who had been initially enthusiastic were long gone. Although the board was told that a key reason for giving the contract to Raytheon was that they had with them a man who had over two decades of experience in PRT, the board was not to be swayed by Anderson's logic, and instead brought in various transportation "experts" to help them with the planning. The only manner in which transportation experts could gain practical operational experience was in the existing transportation systems: heavy rail, light rail, subways, buses and monorails. So they could be expected to bring a decided bias to the deliberations. Also, the RTA people proved that the "not invented here" syndrome was by no means limited to corporations. All of the blame for what happened cannot be laid on Raytheon's doorstep. Within their right to have input, the board of the RTA proceeded to allow certain modifications invented by their Technical Support contractor. The RTA staff failed to supervise adequately this contractor. The consequences were appalling.

One of these modifications was to specify that the vehicles would be four-person cars rather than three-person, as specified by Anderson's Taxi 2000 design. This meant an extra bench seat. A three-person car is entirely adequate, as the average ridership, as in automobiles, is about 1.1 persons per car. Among Anderson's more than 90 technical papers is one which carefully delineates the reasons why a three-passenger car is the optimum size. Chief among these reasons is that a car capable of holding more passengers will have to be longer and hence heavier, which affects guideway strength, berth size in stations, station size and therefore total costs.

Anderson's design had always included provision for the handicapped; every car was a handicapped car, and would accept a wheelchair. The RTA authorities liked this provision, but in their flawless sagacity, bolstered by a committee of experts on the handicapped, they mandated that the wheelchair must be able to face forward, rather than positioned sideways in the car as specified by Anderson. The harm to the design, not obvious at first, was enormous. This required that the vehicle be three feet longer than if the wheelchair remained sideways. This increased the weight of the car substantially, increased the headway distance by over three feet, required longer station berths and hence larger stations, and a stronger guideway to support the heavier cars. It is doubtful that the RTA had any idea of what havoc they were causing, and Raytheon apparently did not advise them, because the provision stuck.

But the changes which Raytheon imposed were even more ghastly. Anderson's design called for the vehicle body to be supported from a cluster of wheels operating within the enclosed guideway, some running on vertical surfaces to provide lateral stability. The Raytheon engineers opted instead for a 4-wheel automotive type chassis, running—you guessed it—in a U-shaped guideway, a perfect snow catcher. Had they bothered to explore the literature—Anderson's designs or published papers, the papers of others, or the printed summaries of the several conferences on PRT—they would have learned that this concept had already been proven impractical many times.

The unique guideway design for which Anderson is credited provides for a compact unit, approximately three feet square in size, with a slot at the top through which the struts bearing the vehicle cabin extend. This precludes most snow accumulation, and any snow which enters through the slot falls out harmlessly through the open bottom of the guideway. Icicles do not form. Thus the Taxi 2000 design is an all-weather, all-climate design, suitable for any city in the world. The Raytheon design, by contrast, could not have been better designed to collect and retain snow. The engineers belatedly realized that snow-melting equipment was going to be necessary to deal with this problem. No provision was made for icicles which might form if this melted snow re-froze, causing a potential hazard. One of Anderson's students who worked on the problem calculated that the cost of melting the snow was several times that of propelling the vehicles. By now, the efficiency of the cars had been reduced to less than that of the automobile.

The Raytheon engineers decided that linear induction motors were unsuitable for various reasons, and so opted instead for conventional electric motors driving the wheels through gearing. Here again, if they had looked they would have found that linear induction motors had been profitably validated by several experimenters successfully using test tracks. Perhaps as a result of these early experiments, thousands of linear induction motors have been in daily operation for many years. In the Raytheon design, braking through the wheels was not dependable; the wheels could slip under conditions where snow and ice prevail on the running surfaces. This problem was discovered during the design phase, and it was then found necessary to apply a carborundum coating to the steel running plates, in order to improve the coefficient of friction. The coating, of course, added substantially to the design cost, and also in actual practice would need periodic replacement.

One of the most flagrant examples of the "not invented here" syndrome was the design of an onboard switch which consisted of several cylinder-operated components, instead of using the simple, single-member element of Anderson's design. After paying for his patent, Raytheon inexplicably didn't use it.

All of these changes added weight to the vehicles and hence to the guideway; the Raytheon engineers would have to completely redesign the guideway. Even before the vehicle design was settled, Raytheon substituted a three-foot diameter pipe section on which were mounted the components of the U-shaped guideway. The blame for this cannot be laid entirely on the engineers. Taxi 2000 has learned from a reliable source that the use of the pipe was mandated from higher up; the engineers had no choice. A Raytheon subsidiary, based in Idaho, manufactures large pipes for the oil industry. The engineers were told to use this pipe.

Rather than working with Taxi 2000 to use its existing control, the Raytheon engineers stubbornly decided to invent their own control system for the project. They are reputed to have spent millions and to have had a large number of engineers working on this, but the final product was not so good as the Taxi 2000 control system.

All of these changes visited ruination upon the carefully budgeted $40 million forecast for the testing phase. Disillusionment may have already began to set in with the RTA, as they did not contribute much more than their agreed-upon half to the project. Raytheon, however, now obligated beyond recall, continued to pour untold sums into the development until the testing was finally consummated, two years beyond the target date.

Jerry Kieffer, in his critique of the manuscript, offers further perspective:

> Just before the Raytheon-belly-up on PRT 2000, a media spokesperson at the RTA told me that in the last year of the RTA/Raytheon partnership, RTA members watched with alarm the growing cost of the joint project. Even though the RTA definitely limited its cost participation in the project, members of the RTA board concerned with inadequately funded bus and rail operations feared that the PRT project would use up too much of the RTA's resources and deprive the bus and rail operations of vitally needed rehabilitation funds and funds for new equipment. She also said that the

Mayor of Rosemont procrastinated on coming up with a business plan (required by the RTA) that spelled out where Rosemont would get the funds for its share of the costs. Part of his problem was that he was counting on revenues from a new Indian-run gambling casino, and authority to have another gambling casino in that part of Illinois required approval of the legislature and the governor.

During all this time, the RTA maintained a position of backing the development to the hilt. Their newsletters were full of glowing accounts of the development and what it would portend for the future. The chairman, Tom McCracken, clearly wanted the project to succeed, as did others on the board. They had retained the right in the contract, however, either to accept or reject the development.

Taxi 2000 was effectively kept out of decision-making during the entire process. But during this whole time, great care was taken by the Taxi 2000 team not to cast any aspersions on the development. But others in the emerging field of PRT had no such reservations. Raytheon was making some effort to sell the product to other interested parties here and abroad, and in every case the design was rejected as being too heavy, large and expensive. These expressions of distaste were not limited to being visited upon the Raytheon sales force. It is quite evident that the tacit worldwide rejection of the Raytheon PRT-2000 system was not lost on the Chicago RTA authorities.

The RTA Reaction

The testing was completed in the spring of 1998, and the RTA was invited to review and ride on this new transportation in which they had had a definitive role. The reaction seemed to have been cautiously optimistic, and the press was advised that the RTA would be voting on it in September. The Chicago papers ran feature articles complete with pictures of this new wonder.

September came and went with no action. The Taxi 2000 team waited with baited breath; it stood to benefit under the terms of the agreement. Then October and the following months of the year came and went in succession, with no action. November was the high water mark. The team began to receive hints from well-placed sources that the project would not be accepted. It was said that Rosemont did not have the necessary funds to finance the system. The RTA assumed the posture of not being able to help beyond a minimum sum, with the excuse that its funds were tied to other transportation investments which had to be honored in order to insure the receipt of matching Federal funds. Finally, well into 1999, it became common knowledge what had happened. The project was simply allowed to die on the vine. No vote was ever taken.

In contrast to the previous glowing descriptions, the current newsletters of the RTA made no further mention of personal rapid transit. The RTA advertised they were hosting a convention on transportation in 1999. PRT was not on the agenda; it was not mentioned at all.

By the fall of 1999, it was obvious to everyone including Raytheon that the PRT-2000 design for the Chicago Regional Transportation Authority was going nowhere. Raytheon had suffered some painful reverses in the value of its stock as a result of this and other more serious problems. In October, 1999, they issued a news release in which they stated that they were "exiting the personal rapid transit business".

The advocates of PRT now had two strikes against them: the Morgantown fiasco and the abortive failure of the Ratheon initiative.

Many lessons were learned from this encounter with Raytheon. Obviously, Taxi 2000 will not repeat the same mistakes again. Control can not be allowed slip from the hands of Ed Anderson and Taxi 2000, and the "not invented here" monster must not be allowed to escape from its cage. Taxi 2000 had for some time been engaged in legal sparring with Raytheon in an effort to become disengaged from their restrictive contract. With the termination of Raytheon's ill-fated effort in the PRT field, this objective was realized without a great deal of additional hassle.

And what of the $20 million of taxpayer's money spent by the RTA to design and test the system? Down the drain. Although it was not the initial intention, the conclusion of the RTA board seemed to be that the expenditure was just a necessary outlay to prove that the highly-touted development known as PRT was not viable.

Chapter 8

The Entrenchment .

The Perceived Threat

It is axiomatic that new ideas in any field threaten careers and business. The threat of PRT is no exception; it is normal for people to fear that their jobs may be done away with if a new development such as PRT occurs. PRT has such remarkable and clear advantages over all other forms of transportation that it is little wonder that existing hierarchies imagine themselves under threat. Because of the obvious advantages, the *perceived* threat to existing jobs and corporations posed by PRT may be far more extensive than that of other evolving industries.

Such fears, however, are not well founded. Even the most avid enthusiasts of PRT do not claim that it will replace any existing form of transportation. What PRT may accomplish as it comes into maturity and widespread use is to slow or stop the unbridled expansion of other forms of transportation, most notably the automobile, and, thereby, provide far better public transportation and help to reduce pollution and congestion.

From the beginning, the role of the railroads has been that of an adversary. The bureaucrats of existing railroad systems appear to believe that development of any alternate form of transportation would be to their detriment. This state of affairs prevails not only in the U.S. but in other countries as well. For example, the promising German PRT development, Cabintaxi, was given a near deathblow by powerful railroad interests; then, while it was still reeling, the mortal injury was administered by the German government.

The promoters of planned railroad facilities seem particularly paranoid in this regard, particularly those concerned with the implementation of so-called "light rail" systems. The name, "light rail", incidentally, seems to imply that the cars and tracks are lighter in weight than those of conventional railroad equipment, which might create the impression in the minds of many that the system is less expensive. In practice, there is little distinction. Railroad passenger cars of greatly varying weight have been in service for many years, depending on whether or not aluminum was used for construction. Many "light rail" cars being proposed today are heavier than "heavy rail" cars.

An Example of Entrenchment

One would think that public transportation systems, being essentially governmental bodies having the common good as their goal, would not be prone to stoop to measures designed to harass competitors and even to put them out of business. However, Catherine Burke, in her extensive work titled *Innovation and Public Policy*, has documented many such cases. One example she gives is in regard to the emergence of the jitney.

Jitneys were modified five or six-passenger automobiles which were in operation in some cities as early as 1910, then charging a five cent fare. Jitneys followed semiflexible routes which could be altered to deliver the passenger as close to his destination as possible. Thus it had many of the desirable characteristics of personal transportation. While you had to wait until one came along and it might make a few other stops, you stood a good chance of getting near your destination; there was no standing, no transfers, and you only had to know your destination.

This was clearly an advantage over the streetcar and the electrified railway, so it quickly gained in popularity. The jitneys began to cut into the ridership and the profits of these repositories of the public trust. By 1917, it was estimated that there were 24,000 jitneys in operation in the United States. Something would have to be done about these upstarts, who seemed to think that the free enterprise system allowed encroachment upon the profits of duly established public conveyances.

Then, as ever, the railroad interests had tremendous clout. In nearly every state having jitneys the railroads were able to persuade legislators to pass restrictive legislation of various kinds. This varied all the way from restrictions on certain routes to outright designation of the jitney as an illegal enterprise. In many areas jitneys are outlawed to this day. Looking back, it is hard to believe the fact that these laws were put on the books between 1914 and 1920, during the first world war. Such was the passion of the vested interests in protecting "their rights". The laws were not only confiscatory, they were arduously enforced. The jitneys were effectively legislated out of business.

Light Rail

It is unfortunately true that light rail is one of the most expensive and least cost-effective of all forms of transportation. This is not from the biased viewpoint of the promoters of PRT. Independent agencies have shown conclusively, in study after study of systems that have been in place for a number of years, that light rail does nothing to reduce congestion or the number of people who use automobiles.

Even a book devoted to the interests of conventional rail transit systems and their potential, *Urban Rail in America*, by Boris S. Pushkarev and his colleagues at the Regional Plan Association, published in 1982, admits the superiority of the emerging technology. The aim of their book was to develop criteria for fixed guideway transit systems. Yet among their conclusions may be found the following statement:

> With respect to downtown peoplemovers, the findings point to the need for light, single-beam systems that would be less costly to build, obstruct less view, and not require any snow-melting. When developed, such systems could have wide potential use, not limited to downtown circulation. In fact, an "overhead streetcar" on a single-beam guideway could easily pre-empt most of the light rail and and peoplemove market defined here, and some of the rapid transit market.

One of the earliest investigations were the HUD studies, as they came to be known, done by the Stanford Research Institute and the General Research Corporation, under a grant from UMTA, The Urban Mass Transportation Administration. These studies, released in 1968, showed that, with the projected growth in population and use of automobiles, if only conventional transit systems were developed, the problems of cities would continue to worsen. Only by developing completely new systems would it be possible to reverse the direction of the worsening congestion in our cities.

Even if built, people don't care to ride existing public transportation. Conventional bus and rail transit worldwide has been losing steadily to the automobile, and in the United States now constitutes less than three per cent of the urban trips.

Notwithstanding the clear evidence to the contrary, proponents of light rail continue to promote these systems, and to combat any suggestions that alternative concepts ought to be given consideration. The lobbies for the conventional rail industry have succeeded on many occasions in blocking attempts to study any alternatives. They have done this on the local level with city officials, on the state level with legislators, and on the federal level with various agencies of the federal government. For example, after the successful implementation of the Morgantown system, the lobbies for conventional transit were effective in killing the UMTA High-Capacity PRT program in September 1974. Even developers of other advanced transportation systems conspired against PRT; Otis and Westinghouse testified against the UMTA High-Capacity PRT program.

There have been many attempts to change this mental attitude, but they have fallen on deaf ears. University of Minnesota Economist Professor Herbert Mohring stated, "I know of no economist of any distinction who studies transport problems who regards rail transit as sensible anywhere in the United States."

One of the main reasons this state of affairs persists is the fact that the Federal government over many years has offered various programs which provide funding for the construction of transportation systems of *proven* technology. Politicians and bureaucrats at many levels see their own state or community as the recipient of substantial funding which means jobs for their citizens and business for the economy if conventional transportation is used. Conventional transit offers immediate return, but new systems offer only an uncertain return at an unknown future date.

Many advocates of PRT remember bitterly how Federal control of the purse strings resulted in perverting the design at Morgantown into something grossly different from PRT. They know that once the government gets control, almost anything can happen, and they are not entirely sanguine about seeking Federal funding. The proponents of railroad practice, in contrast, have no such concerns. Their technology dates from the nineteenth century. It is completely established and solidified. They have nothing to fear from government manipulation of the science.

The lengths to which some public officials have gone to garner this Federal money is astonishing. They ignore the many studies which clearly show that in very few cases has light rail proved to be advantageous. They suppress the fact that *all* present forms of public transportation have to be heavily subsidized to remain solvent.

It is usually not necessary to denigrate PRT, because the level of public awareness is so low that this alternative is seldom raised. But, if required, some do not hesitate to cast aspersions upon PRT, stating that it is unproven, unsafe, unsightly, and more expensive. The only truth of which is that it is unproven (and this is only true as to actual installations, the concept having been proven repeatedly in test trials). Without any documentation, they make claims that the cost of construction and operation of PRT systems would be higher than light rail, which assumption is simply a falsehood.

PRT Costs Extensively Studied

The cost of PRT has been exhaustively researched. It is probably one of the few industries which has received this amount of research *prior to implementation*. The average total cost of a modern PRT system is about 40 cents per vehicle-mile or passenger-mile at this date, compared to 50 cents for the automobile, and a wide range of from $2 to $6 per passenger-mile for light rail. So the truth is that light rail is at least 4 times as expensive as PRT, and can be much more than that.

Regarding safety, the fact is, light rail is the technology which should be called unsafe. Compelled by its very nature to involve numerous grade crossings, light rail has compiled a quite dismal record from the operating histories of actual installations. According to federal records, these systems kill about three times as many people as bus systems. In the Denver light rail system, according to Andre Hudson, RTD spokesman at Denver, collisions on the system average about one per week, one of which was fatal each year. Hudson said Denver's experience is typical for cities of that size having light rail. As another example, Portland has had five fatalities in 1999. The weight and momentum of the train of vehicles combine to deepen the damage to property and loss of lives.

Another aspect of safety, not often mentioned, is that a PRT station does not have the potential hazard of a deep pit along the station platform, as with subways and other train stations. Passengers of these facilities have sometimes fatally fallen (or suicidally jumped) into the path of a train. If they are not killed by a train, they could suffer broken bones from the fall, or be electrocuted by the third rail. In contrast, the top of the PRT guideway is only a small distance below the station platform, so that a normal person having inadvertently stepped off the platform could easily climb out. The electric power rails are protected by the design of the guideway. Electrocution would be highly unlikely, even if a leg went through the narrow guideway slot.

The vested interests and their lobbyists have been successful in casting doubt upon the ability of any new form of transportation to solve our problems. They have done this at all levels of government. The true extent of the delay this has caused may never be known.

In truth, it is the author's belief that the true facts have never been brought to light. Now that PRT is a reality and is virtually unstoppable, it does not seem improper to reveal the role which adverse publicity and lobbying has played.

In contrast, the forces of PRT have been quite innocuous. They have never been organized into anything resembling a group characterized by unanimity in thought, let alone in political will. Nor have they ever had the money necessary to pursue political objectives. The only organizations fostering PRT are the Advanced Transit Association (ATRA), which must by its nature promote *all* forms of advanced transportation, and Citizens for PRT (CPRT). Neither has ever indulged in any lobbying activities at the Federal level. At the state level, CPRT is making noble effort to acquaint the members of the Minnesota legislature with the benefits of PRT. The fact is, the proponents of PRT have exercised remarkable restraint in the face of all the negative publicity with which they have been faced. The forces of PRT are not out to trash anyone else's form of transportation. They simply want PRT to get a fair shake. Our spread-out metropolitan areas need more service-effective modes of transit, and at much lower cost. The proponents of PRT want a fair shake at providing this.

Chapter 9

The PRT Experience

A Lovely Ride

In Chapter Two it was stated that *every one* of the items on our wish-list of desirable features of a new transportation system was fulfilled by the technology of the transportation renaissance. The actual experience of using PRT is pleasant one to contemplate. Put yourself into this scenario:

Arriving at any station on the network at any time of the day or night, any day of the year, you will gain access to the second floor level via a stairway or elevator. It is possible that because of existing or manmade land contours, you may be at the operating level of the system when you arrive.

You purchase a ticket for your destination for a modest fare from an automatic vendor. Your destination is all you need to know. You don't have to select the proper route, look for a certain track, or watch for a certain designated car. Any car is the right car. There will be large-scale illuminated maps of the system to show you which destination station is within closest walking distance of your goal.

You proceed to the berthing track where the vehicles, running on cushioned rubber tires, are quietly arriving and departing. Normally, at non-rush hours, there will be a vehicle there waiting for you. You insert your ticket into a slot in a stanchion by the car you have chosen. If there are several cars waiting, you will chose the one at the front, as it will depart first. At the busiest times, you may have to wait up to a minute or two for a vehicle to come. It may be an empty, whereupon you get right in, or it may have an occupant, who will need to exit first. Your encoded ticked automatically informs the onboard computer and other system computers of your destination. Before you have even taken your seat, the computers have identified the most effective route to your destination.

The cars run in one direction only, like a one-way street. While there are some PRT proponents still promoting two-way systems, most designers have accepted the reality that one-way systems are substantially simpler to design and build, and therefore less costly. But how do you get to a station which may be one or two stops "upstream", or the wrong direction, from your boarding station? The answer is, you need to go around the loop until you come to it, just as you would in automobile traffic in a city with many one-way streets. This will only take a few minutes.

PRT networks consist of many of these loops tied together with switches, called merge and diverge points in PRT jargon. By traveling around these loops, you can get to any station on the network. (These points are always switches, never crossings.) It seems complicated, but, remember, you don't have to worry about it. The computers have it figured out for your car before you leave your boarding station, and continuously monitor your route to ensure it is the best one (there may be several possible routes in a large network). The final route will be determined as you approach each diverge point.

Unless you are accompanied by one or two family members or friends, you will normally travel alone. Your ticket price is for the destination, and is the same fare regardless of whether one person rides, or two or three persons travel together. You can split the fare if you so arrange with other passengers, such as with fellow employees. Normally, however, you may not easily find someone going to your destination at the same time.

You are always assured of a seat. There is plenty of room for shopping purchases or even suitcases on the floor in front of you. If you are in a wheelchair, you will be just as speedily accommodated as anyone else. Every car is a wheelchair car. It is easy to wheel yourself aboard; the car floor and the platform are at the same level. A friend can take the next car and arrive just after you do.

The door will close and the car will move smoothly out onto the mainline when, and only when, there is a suitable space available. Usually there will be no delay. Cars moving along the main line may slip back a certain amount to create such a space, decelerating almost imperceptibly. This same slipping back may occur at all merge points on the system. The speed of travel on the mainline will probably be about 35 miles per hour. Once on the main line, your car will go past all other stations along the way; you will never stop until you arrive at your destination. You never transfer to another car.

Your vehicle is an all-weather car, equipped with automatic heating, ventilation, and air-conditioning. The PRT cars are non-poluting. There are no fumes, and there is no noise or jerkiness. You can read, rest, enjoy the view, or work on your laptop. If there should be a blinding snowstorm outside, with zero visibility, the automatic computer-controlled functions will not be affected in the slightest, and will take you unerringly to your destination, functioning just as well as on a sunny day.

Since you never travel with anyone else except by choice, your safety is assured. If someone should force himself into your car, you can immediately leave the car, or call for help on the car's intercom. Surveillance personal will take appropriate action, at either the initiating station or the destination.

It is possible, but quite unlikely, that you might look out and see that the lights in the area over which you are passing are out, due to a power failure. If so, the system may have automatically switched to standby power, in which mode it can run indefinitely; you would not have felt the changeover.

After you have overcome any lingering trepidation you may harbor over the fact that there are no human beings directly involved with your destiny, you can settle back and enjoy the ride. In fact, the computers to which the job has been delegated are far more competent in making the required decisions than human operators ever possibly could be. Then, too, you remember that a grade crossing accident with a car, truck or train is impossible, since the system is elevated above these. It is also impossible for a crossing collision with another PRT car to occur, since the system never crosses itself. Looking straight down for twenty feet to the ground may seem a little unsettling at first, until you remember that the design is such that it is impossible for the car to derail or tip over.

The vehicle has taken the most efficient route over the network to your destination station. You may have never been there before, which is irrelevant; you don't need to recognize your station or do anything to ensure that the car will stop. It will automatically switch off the main line, decelerate as it approaches the station, and come to a stop in the berthing area, either as the first car in line or behind one or more other cars. The door will open and you will alight.

Your trip has been completed economically, expeditiously, safely, comfortably, quietly, and free of worry or concern or tension-raising factors. You have no parking problem, and you are within a few minutes walk of your final destination. What could be nicer? After you have ridden on the system several times and realized how convenient, safe, economical, non-intimidating and pleasant it really is, you will wonder how you ever got along without it.

Chapter 10

The Downsides

The Wave-off

No one but an unmitigated optimist could imagine that any development conceived by man could be completely free of any negative factors. Such an accomplishment cannot be obtained in the real world in which we live, nor would it be desirable. There are tradeoffs which must be considered in every endeavor. PRT is no exception. Not even to mention these would be a disservice to any interested reader. Yet it is true that those tradeoffs which occur are of such minor nature that they seem almost trivial. There are few inventions of history with such a favorable outlook.

Loading berths consist of a series of spaces on the station track into which the cars come to rest, one behind the other. Each station will have a designated number of berths, depending on the required throughput, or vehicles per unit of time through the station. As the forward-most car receives a passenger and departs, each car in turn moves up to the next berth.

One of the conditions which can occur in any projected PRT system, is that, on rare occasions, all of the loading berths at any given station can become completely full. This might consist of empty cars waiting for passengers, and loaded cars waiting for an opening on the main line to depart. This by itself causes no difficulty, but if an occupied car approaches, bound for that station, there will not be room to accommodate the car.

The computers, of course, are cognizant of the situation, and the message is transmitted to the car that it cannot enter; it must continue to proceed along on the main line. This is known in PRT technology as a "wave-off". Thus, if you are happily riding along in your PRT vehicle approaching your destination, and you suddenly realize that your station just went whizzing by, you have been subjected to a wave-off.

This condition is a tradeoff because it would be possible to minimize this situation by making the stations larger and larger, creating more and more berths, the possibility of a wave-off becoming more and more unlikely. The possibility begins to approach zero asymptotically, as a mathematician might say. Well, then, why not make the stations large enough so that this hardly ever happens? It's a matter of cost. Every additional foot of station size means additional investment. In a large network, this could literally mean millions of dollars of extra cost.

But what happens to you after you just went whizzing by your station? Do you continue to ride endlessly on the system, like "The Man Who Never Returned", in a song popular a few years back about a man who couldn't exit the subway because he didn't have the fare, and so rode on forever, piling up a fortune in unpaid fares? ("He rode forever 'neath the streets of Boston, he's the man who never returned.") Or does your vehicle just take you back to your originating point, and let you off?

The answer, of course, is neither of these extremes. Large networks consist of many loops tied together. As you whizzed by your desired station, and as you pass each diverge point, the computers will take you back to your destination by the most expeditious route. On a smaller network, you may have to go around a fairly substantial distance, but within a few minutes you will come around again, and the chances of another wave-off are very slim. Empty cars are not allowed to accumulate at a station to the point where they fill all berths, causing a wave-off. If there are too many empties, some of them are are sent to a destination which is low on empties.

On most simulations which have been completed for various cities, the number of cars which are waved-off is no more than one tenth of one per cent, or one chance out of 1,000. It has been suggested that a prize of some sort be awarded as compensation to any customer who actually encounters a wave-off!

Routing of Empty Cars

One of the concerns about PRT is that there are always a considerable number of empty cars cruising the main line (typically about one third of the cars), which seems to indicate that the system is not very efficient. But all forms of public transportation have this condition. Busses and trains, for example, return nearly empty to metropolitan areas in order to serve the rush hour patronage. PRT will operate in a similar manner. Empty PRT cars must be sent continuously to those stations which are low on empties, to accommodate arriving patrons. Some stations may receive quite a number cars with passengers at nearly the same time. After these passengers exit, the station berthing track will have more empties than normal. These will be routed automatically to stations which have a shortage. Here again, the computer is indispensable, easily performing a job which would be beyond the ability of a human being.

The computers in the systems are what is known as dual-redundant. This means there are two identical linked computers for each job, not only in every car but also all wayside computers. These computers continuously monitor each other for failure, and if one should fail, the other will take over the functions and send a signal that the pair needs replacement.

Wait Period

PRT is touted as the transportation technology in which "you don't wait for the vehicle to come along, the vehicle waits for you to come along". Well, maybe. But here again we encounter a tradeoff. It is technically possible to design a PRT system in which the amount of time which passengers spend waiting for a car approaches zero. By increasing the number of berths at all stations, and the total number of cars on the system, it is theoretically possible to eliminate almost all waiting.

In the final analysis, it comes down to what is really practical. Those small increments of waiting time as zero waiting is approached come at a very high cost in system components. From a practical standpoint, it is far more sensible to accept a small waiting period, especially during rush hour periods.

The program for the city of Rochester, Minnesota, to serve the famous Mayo clinic and its related hospitals, is a fascinating development which may become one of the first actual PRT installations. In the course of developing this program, Dr. Anderson was asked whether it would be possible to design a system in which the waiting time would not exceed one minute. The standard answer, of course, is that normally a passenger does not wait at all; there is usually an empty car at the station, waiting for him. But to give a ready answer as to whether, when no car was waiting, any passenger should have to wait more than one minute was not something that could be given off the top of his head. He responded that it might be possible to get fairly close to this stipulation.

To answer this question, in his simulation of the Rochester layout, Dr. Anderson developed a series of calculations in which this requirement was one of the parameters. He was able to show that waiting time would be under one minute about 98 per cent of the time, and seldom, if ever, over one and one-half minutes. This was acceptable to the City of Rochester and the Mayo clinic authorities.

A small but appreciable amount of waiting is going to be an integral part of PRT service. When it is considered that this is only the unusual condition, and, even so, the waiting period will probably be on the order of one or two minutes, it does not seem like a very serious detriment. Compared with all other forms of public transportation, where waiting is a fact of life, it is insignificant.

Guideway Beauty

It has been alleged by some detractors that the guideways of a PRT system are unsightly. Some people express this opinion without really understanding what the guideway of a modern PRT system is like. They hark back to their recollection of having seen the track construction of the Chicago or New York elevated train systems, which are so large that they darken the street underneath, and assume PRT must be something like that. Or they may have seen or at least heard about the mammoth guideway required for the Morgantown installation, which is often erroneously referred to as "PRT". Even the guideway for the successfully tested Raytheon PRT-2000 system was large and ponderous.

In truth, the guideways of the modern designs of PRT systems are nothing like these examples. They are slim, compact designs, approximately three feet square in cross section. Delicately spanning the sixty feet between typical columns, they are far from being an eyesore.

The judgment as to the esthetic quality of a PRT guideway is and always will be a subjective one. To one who feels that any intrusion into the clear space above the ground is an affront, guideways will always seem objectionable. To an engineer who appreciates the nuances of guideway design, they will be beautiful.

Beauty is in the eye of the beholder; in the case of PRT guideways, this is certainly true. But the question of whether or not the guideways are aesthetically acceptable pales into insignificance when compared with other aspects of the urban scene. Anyone who claims that PRT guideways are unsightly must also object to skyway walkways which cross the downtown streets now in many of our cities. His objection must be all the more vigorous, since the skyways are much larger. Of far greater consequence is the question of whether the architecture of our cities is in good taste. In this area, we can probably find a great many opinions, but there is probably a strong consensus that certain buildings are not attractive, and that a few are downright ugly. Such eyesores certainly exert a far greater effect upon the beauty of our cities than that which will be produced by the slim elevated guideways of a modern PRT system.

Chapter 11

Pollution and Energy

Pollution

In Chapter Two, our "wish list" of desirable features for an ideal transit system, we posited that the system should be far less polluting than all other forms of conventional transportation. To some this may have been seen to be a worthy goal, but probably not terribly important. Here is another example of how conventional wisdom may go far astray in the case of an unknown entity. Because, far from being not terribly important, the pollution aspects of personal rapid transit are among the most salient. The pollution aspects of PRT really are of major significance.

New ground-breaking developments in the automotive industry portend great improvement in the pollution levels of the cars of the future. Some questionable ideas, such as compressed air or flywheels, are being seriously promoted. Other seemingly more practical solutions, such as better fuel efficiency, the electric car, the advent of the hybrid vehicle which combines a smaller internal combustion engine with electric propulsion, all signal a welcome reduction in pollution. The fuel cell car which will run on hydrogen will, when it is finally commercialized, produce zero pollution.

Unfortunately, all of these solutions, while they make worthy strides toward reduction of particulate emissions which account for much of our smog and health problems, do nothing to address the fundamental problem with the automobile: *there are too many*

89

of them. In fact, the very attractiveness of the highly-touted new models of the future will only intensify the problems. The freeways and streets will become more clogged, congestion will worsen, parking will be an even greater nightmare.

To achieve its place in the sun, PRT must consist of a program of low pollution which can be verified readily and which can be delivered unerringly. In its claim to be utterly different from railroads and busses, it must make a clean break with the typical sources of power of conventional transportation.

Energy

The clean break which PRT must make with typical sources of power is accomplished by powering the cars electrically. In this respect, it makes the same break with fossil fuels that the electric automobile does. However, one should not make the mistake of equating each electric-powered PRT vehicle with each electric automobile expected to be on the roads. They are far from similar; PRT vehicles will use only a small fraction of the power of an electric automobile.

The reasons for this are manifold. Firstly, the PRT cars are much smaller, so the energy needed to power them is less, even though linear induction motors are not so efficient as rotary motors. Secondly, the cars are much lighter; they are not required to carry the heavy batteries which are an integral part of the electric auto. Thirdly, and this is probably the most important point, the acceleration needed is reduced. This is particularly significant since the amount of mass to be accelerated is less.

A little digression may be useful in respect to this last point. Any student of physics should recall that to accelerate any mass up to a given speed requires the expending of energy. It may seem strange to the uninitiated, but to maintain that object at the given speed requires no energy at all in the absence of friction. Thus a ball once set in motion on a flat lever surface would continue rolling along at the same speed indefinitely, without any further help, if it were not for the attenuating forces of friction, such as contact with the air and the indentation of the surfaces of contact, however slight.

The acceleration forces required in much of our transportation industry are actually quite amazing. It is said that a fully loaded airliner on a typical flight consumes nearly half of its fuel in accelerating the plane from the runway up to cruising speed at 35,000 feet or so. The advantage, of course, is that it has to do this only once per flight.

A PRT vehicle shares this same advantage with an airliner. It only has to accelerate once, out of its berth at any given station up to main line speed, where it will cruise at practically the same speed for its entire trip until it decelerates into its destination station. And here it gains another advantage. Thanks to the technology of electro-magnetic braking, it will actually put some of the energy of its initial acceleration back into the power grid as it decelerates to a stop. This is not to imply that the PRT vehicle will not require energy to reach its destination. Climbing the grades of the system, changing speed as required at merge points, and overcoming friction will all require energy. But that energy will be far less than that required by a conventional vehicle.

In contrast, an electric auto will have to accelerate up to speed after each stop at a traffic light, or each slow-down or stop due to congested roads. These stops can add up to quite a few instances on a typical trip. This is why an electric car can go more miles before recharging on the highways even at higher speeds than it can in congested city driving. Every time a car passes another car, heavy acceleration forces also come into play. PRT has no such extremes; no PRT vehicle ever passes another vehicle.

We have been comparing here the electric auto, which is the most efficient automobile, with the electric PRT vehicle. What about today's conventional internal combustion cars? How do they stack up? They do miserably, as one might expect, compared to

PRT vehicles. Automobiles, being much heavier, take far more energy to come up to speed. Their larger size creates more friction moving through the airstream, regardless of streamlining. The energy they use, of course, comes from burning fossil fuels, which is highly polluting. They obviously suffer the same disadvantages as the electric auto at each stop for traffic lights or congestion. But the electric car has one major advantage over the internal combustion automobile: it does not pollute while the car is waiting for a traffic light. Conventional autos produce untold tons of particle emission every day in every city, waiting by the millions with engines idling at traffic lights in the U. S. and throughout the world.

PRT, in contrast, has no such limitation. The vehicle does not stop at all on its way to its destination, and even if it did, no fossil fuel would be burned and no pollution caused.

A measure of the difference between conventional autos and PRT cars may be seen in the amount of horsepower necessary to power the respective vehicles. It is not uncommon to see autos rated at 200 to 250 horsepower. Compare this with what is required for a PRT vehicle. 20 to 25 horsepower, thank you, will do the job nicely—a factor of ten to one.

Pollution: Other Aspects

An astute observer would certainly raise the point that, although the PRT vehicles are electric, the pollution effect of the *generation* of that electricity could vary widely, perhaps to the serious detriment of PRT as a non-polluter. This is a valid position. The main argument against it is that far less energy is needed to power the PRT vehicles than autos or trains. As indicated above, the horsepower requirements of a PRT vehicle are only one tenth that of a typical automobile. But we must include the energy used in accelerating from traffic light and congestion stops, and for passing other cars, as well as the energy used up in idling at traffic light and congestion stops. This is difficult to estimate, but could easily run another factor of ten. So it probably is safe to say that the typical PRT vehicle uses only one twentieth as much power as a typical automobile.

Smokestacks of electrical generating plants usually are considerably less polluting than auto exhaust emissions per unit of energy. With the advent of requirements which have been legislated, such as the mandatory installation of scrubbers and other pollution controls, the history of pollution from the power plants gradually has been changing for the better. There are now certain vast areas of the West wherein the haze which has been accumulating over decades has abated, and the air clarity is restored almost to that of the days of old. It is now possible on good days again to see clearly across the colossal valleys and canyons, and view the mountain vistas. In other places, however, the smog is reported to be worse than ever.

Some power plants are now changing over, either voluntarily or by state-mandated policies, to renewable resources such as wind or solar to power a part of their production. To the extent that such production is in place, pollution is further reduced.

Such considerations raise an interesting alternative. If a PRT system was designed and built for which the primary source of power was electricity generated by one or more system-owned power plants which used non-polluting renewable resources as their energy source, the PRT system itself would be truly non-polluting. In such a case, the system undoubtedly would use the local power company as its source of standby power. The only condition under which such a system would contribute any pollution would be when it was necessary to switch over to standby power.

Another objectionable by-product of conventional transportation is now commonly being accepted as pollution: *noise*. Even avid railroad buffs have to admit that trains are loud. Buses are not particularly quiet, either. And they emit smelly fumes which may be toxic and are quite unwelcome. In contrast, the linear electric motors of PRT vehicles are extremely quiet. There is no gear noise because there are no gears. The vehicles use rubber cushioned tires running on steel surfaces, instead of steel on steel as in railroad practice.

In summary, PRT vehicles are far more attractive from a minimum pollution viewpoint than railroads, buses, or any of the practical new automotive designs which are being highly touted. The goal of PRT is not to replace the automobile; this would not be practical nor desirable. But every trip made in a PRT vehicle will result in far less pollution than the same trip made in an automobile, even those of advanced design.

Pollution and energy consumption are not the only global problems we face. Declining water quality and availability, soil erosion, global warming, expanding deserts, receding forests are others. As forecast by many authorities, the end of cheap oil will soon be upon us, the precursor of the end of the petroleum age. Since PRT can be built by devoting far fewer resources than those required by other forms of transportation, it makes sound economic and ethical sense to pursue this alternative with great vigor, so that more resources can be devoted to these threats to civilization as we know it.

Chapter 12

Opportunities Unlimited

PRT Fully Developed

It is rather sad in a way, when one stops to think about it, that the entrenched forces of existing forms of transportation so compulsively fear the impact of PRT that they spend a disproportionate amount of time and money opposing it. Far from limiting the opportunities for the development of jobs, engineering, financing, and so on, the advent of PRT *enhances* these chances.

The implementation of the transportation renaissance will spawn a multi-billion dollar industry in cities large and small all over the world. Millions of PRT vehicles will be needed. Thousands of miles of guideways will be erected. Thousands of stations will be built. Once the first successful implementation occurs, the world will never again be the same. People from all over the world will flock to this installation, to see and ride on this new marvel. It will be utterly impossible to install systems fast enough to keep up with the demand.

Every forecast of the potential of PRT, even by the most conservative, quickly gets into billions of dollars. It is probably true that this technology will expand faster than any other form of transportation we have ever known in the industrial age. Steamships, the railroads, the automobile and the airplane all expanded at a rate limited by the slow progress of the evolving technology of each particular form. Although the screw propeller

95

was actually invented first, steamships had to go through the paddlewheel phase before the screw propeller became universal. The railroads went through the arduous process of developing heavier and more powerful steam locomotives. It is only in relatively recent times that the diesel locomotive finally eclipsed the steam engine for all but nostalgic purposes. The automobile and the airplane also went through, and are still going through, long and continuous improvement.

It is difficult to grasp the fact that PRT essentially has already gone through these same developmental steps. PRT has been developed and repeatedly tested and refined, but practically never used, until today the modern PRT concept stands in exactly the same position as the other forms of transportation postulated in the foregoing examples. It is fully designed and ready to go. Starting with Edward Haltom's first monorail concept having PRT attributes, each inventor in his own way has made his own incremental contribution. The successful testings have added further to the growing body of knowledge. For various explainable reasons only a few of these systems were actually built, and then only in a very limited way involving a single instance. This does not alter the fact that the technology has gone through a development period which has resulted in the modern PRT design of today, much the same as it would have if the forerunner systems *had* actually been constructed. Had this occurred, they would have run their course into obsolescence as new and better PRT designs emerged. While the shortcomings would soon have become evident to the owners and users of such systems, they were already known to the most advanced PRT designers, even though they were never built.

It may be helpful to imagine a scenario of what might have happened in regard to steamships and railroads, if somehow the same or similar economic and political forces which have plagued PRT had been operative as these prior forms of transportation developed; in other words, if the forces which prevailed had prevented the actual use of the successive stages of development. Paddlewheelers would have been developed and tested, for example, and they would have proved that ships can readily be propelled through the water by mechanical means. It would not have been necessary for these to be actually *used* before engineers would have perceived that the screw propeller was far superior. Direct steam-engine drive for ships would have been tested, at least by models. Soon the steam-to-electric drive would have been conceived. This too would have been developed, but never used. All of these steps would have added to the growing body of knowledge. Eventually the diesel-electric drive of modern ships would have evolved, which finally would have been accepted by the market place and by political forces.

Similarly, railroad locomotives would have been continuously tested and improved, becoming ever more powerful and efficient, even though no one was willing yet to finance a railroad. It is admittedly quite a stretch to imagine that that final behemoth, the articulated steam locomotive, having two sets of cylinders and driving wheels, could have been invented in advance of actual rail-road practice, but perhaps the point is becoming clear: *PRT technology has already gone through its own development phases!* Just as, in this scenario, the marketplace would have finally recognized the superiority of several modern Diesel locomotives in tandem over even the articulated and then placed its order for the first railroad, the marketplace is now recognizing that PRT must take its place in the history of transportation.

The demand for these prior developing forms of transportation is also a factor here. These other forms more or less kept pace with expanding demand. The railroads in their rush to span the continent tried to keep up with burgeoning demand. The airlines have continued to add routes and destinations over the years as more and more passengers abandoned rail service in favor of the faster air transportation. But never in the history of the world has there existed such a pent-up demand as there will be for PRT. Millions of people worldwide would become potential customers almost instantly if the benefits of PRT could only be made available to them.

Jobs Unbounded

The magnitude of the coming transportation renaissance is such that the U. S. economy will receive a tremendous boost. Opportunities at every level will abound. For a transportation engineer, the possibilities are almost limitless. Rather than being required to continue eking out a survival in existing forms of transportation, the technologies of which date from the late nineteenth and early twentieth centuries, a transportation engineer can ride into the twenty-first century on a new technology. While it is true that PRT is in essence fully designed, there will be immense challenges in designing and laying out new systems for each city or customer. Each will have its peculiar requirements as to curves, merge and diverge points, and station design. When PRT finally takes off, competent transportation engineers will be at a premium.

Computer specialists will be sorely needed. Literally millions and millions of computers will be required. A pair of dual-redundant computers are used in each vehicle. Wayside computers control switching operations. Master computers monitor the entire system. To insure that all of these components are properly programmed and work together properly will require very competent computer experts. This is not to imply that the task is overwhelming. The basic format for these requirements has been established, and in fact is documented each time a full computer simulation is created for a given application. But to create these simulations, many competent computer specialists will be needed.

To the uninitiated, this bewildering computer universe may seem utterly chaotic and beyond attainment. In fact, however, other things are presently being done with computers in our society which exceed the requirements necessary for PRT implementation.

Purchasing agents will be needed to place the contracts for the cities with the vendors who will produce the computer components, the vehicles, guideways, stations and other elements to PRT specifications. Experts will be needed to insure compliance with these specifications, and to coordinate and expedite delivery.

Contractors will be needed to produce all of these elements. It is anticipated that no single manufacturer will be able to produce the volume of vehicles that will be needed, even though the cars are all identical. The challenges here for automated assembly-line manufacturing are immense. A great deal has been done in the automotive industry toward robotic manufacture, even though practically each car produced is different from the one ahead. Many are custom-built to customer requirements. Imagine the possibilities for robotic manufacture when each car is identical. The PRT vehicles will be identical except for such details as interior fabrics, paint jobs, and other cosmetic features, and even so, large production runs of several hundred or more will be exactly alike.

The aluminum and plastics needed for the cars and the steel for the thousands of miles of guideway are not inconsequential. It is anticipated that these industries, from mining, processing, smelting and rolling will enjoy an increase in tonnage produced.

Hundreds of local erection contractors will be needed to erect these guideways. The same is true for the local construction of the stations. Here is an area where substantial variation will occur. Some stations will be within existing buildings, and so will differ markedly from separate exterior stations. The possibilities for design by local architects to harmonize with the existing neighborhoods or urban settings is endless.

Electrical engineering graduates in the field of power generation and distribution will be needed to plan and specify the standby electrical generating plants which can take over automatically in the event of power failure of the local utility. It is conceivable that some PRT systems may be designed to run normally on power generated by their own plants. Such plants could use renewable energy sources, so that the entire system would be in the category of not exhausting our natural resources. In this case, the public utility would serve as the back-up source of power. This concept

has a marked advantage. Since the public utility is always running, the system can be switched almost instantaneously to standby
power. With the reverse design, that is, using the public utility as
the primary power source with diesel-electric generators as standby
power, there is an inevitable time lag representing the time it takes
to get the diesels started and the generators up to speed and on-
line. Any time delay is unacceptable; therefore, battery power would
have to be utilized to fill the gap until the generators were brought
on-line. This represents a sizable investment in batteries and associated gear, and raises the question as to whether batteries alone
would suffice as standby power. Batteries could be charged up at
night at off-peak rates for use either as the normal operating power
source or as standby power.

Planners will be needed at the city level to deal with this new
phenomenon. Each city will, of necessity, be heavily involved with
the proper layout of the system and its initial and ultimate projected size. The city planners will be partners with the PRT experts who can help them make the proper decisions. Land acquisition or air rights can only be negotiated by the city planner and
city authorities. Only the city planner is in a position to cope with
local governing rules with which the system may have to comply.

Not all of the employment needs have been mentioned in this
chapter. The job opportunities are almost endless. The
transportation renaissance will truly usher in a new era of economic
development in our society.

Chapter 13

Avoiding Future Calamity

A Plea for Standards

Since PRT is the world's first transportation technology to be fully developed before being utilized, it is afforded a unique opportunity with which none of the other transportation technologies were blessed. Uniform standards of design could be developed which would apply generally to PRT in the United States, in the Americas, and worldwide. This can be done at the outset, rather than waiting until dissimilar designs of vehicle, guideway, and control methods cause untold waste and delay because of incompatibility.

An example of the value of such standardization can be seen in the case of the railroad system in the United States. People seldom give a second thought to the fact that a given freight car can travel the length and breadth of the country, in fact to any of the 48 contiguous states (and also in Canada and Mexico) without any problem, because the distance between the rails has long been standardized at 4 foot 8 1/2 inches. It is said that this gauge came about because that was the wheel spacing of the carriages since Roman times, which in turn was established by the width of two horses in harness.

This standardization of the track gauge has been a blessing of untold dimensions, but it was not always so. The following description is provided courtesy of A. Scheffer Lang, an energetic proponent of PRT who has had a 50-year career in the nation's railroads and also in key government positions. He is the co-author of several books. His extensive railroad experience is given as Appendix C.

> In New England most of the railroads were built to the 4 feet 8 1/2 inch "standard" gauge that derived from the use of English locomotives, but at the outbreak of the Civil War there were still eleven different gauges in use in the North as a whole. The Erie Railroad, for example, had chosen a gauge of 6 feet so as to keep the traffic of other roads off of their own. In the South most railroads used 5 feet, but even there that gauge was not universal. [George Rogers Taylor, *The Transportation Revolution 1815-1860*, New York (1951), p. 82.]
>
> In 1861 some 46% of the nation's rail mileage was other than standard gauge. The Erie did not shift to standard gauge until 1880, and in that year a fifth of the nation's mileage was still not standard gauge. [John F. Stover, *American Railroads*, second edition, Chicago (1997), p. 143.]
>
> A number of expedients were developed to overcome the problem of disparate gauges at points where freight was moved from one road to the next: "compromise" cars with extra wide wheel treads, cars whose wheels could be slid on their axles, hoisting cars off their trucks (the wheel carriage) and setting them on new ones (a system still in use to interface with Russian 5 foot gauge in Eastern Europe), and three-rail track with idler cars to couple cars of different gauges. None was satisfactory [ibid., p. 143]. This became particularly apparent during the Civil War when the role of the railroads became increasingly important to military operations both in the North and the South. As agricultural products from the Midwest began to ship long distances to East Coast markets the need for more seamless movement also became apparent.
>
> Thus, in the years after the War, railroads began one by

one to convert to standard gauge. This development was given impetus, moreover, by the decision during the War to build the Transcontinental Railroad to standard gauge. By the end of 1880, except for some narrow gauge mileage that was concentrated in the Colorado mountains, almost all of the railroad mileage in the North and West had been converted. In the South, however, there were still more than 12,000 miles of 5-foot gauge. In February of 1886 the Southern railroads came together at a conference in Atlanta and decided the time had come to fall in line, and by the end of 1886 they all had made the conversion to standard gauge. [ibid., pp. 143-144, James E. Vance, Jr. *The North American Railroad*, Baltimore (1995), pp. 113-117.]

It would be sad indeed if we were to allow the same thing to happen with PRT as happened with the railroads. While they finally achieved standardization, the true economic cost as a result of the dissimilarities will never be known. One can argue that, since each city will have its own separate PRT system, it does not matter much whether they all hew to the same standards. This might be true at the outset, though some economies of scale would be sacrificed.

However, as time goes on, the incompatibility monster would begin to rear its ugly head. Cities in the East particularly, which are very close together, will reach a point where it would be desirable to merge certain systems, so that a passenger could travel from a station in city A to another station in city B. If these cities happened to have installed systems which were incompatible, they would be up the creek, as the expression goes. Nothing could be done except to tear out one city's entire system and replace it.

Nor are such conditions peculiar only in the East. Minneapolis and St. Paul provide a good Midwest example. It would be tragic if one could not travel between these two cities on PRT.

Another example is found in the communities of Cincinnati, Covington, and Newport. Fortunately, the foresighted planners of these cities have already begun extensive consultations regarding a comprehensive PRT system to serve the three communities.

We cannot foresee where PRT development will take us. Someday it may be possible to travel considerable distances between cities in a PRT vehicle. Since this is real possibility, it behooves us to establish compatibility standards at the outset in anticipation of the potential problem.

It would be the height of negligence if we made the same mistake that was made with respect to computers and the year 2000 problem, commonly referred to as Y2K. In retrospect, the Y2K problem has come to be regarded as fairly innocuous by the public, but most people do not realize that this is only true because billions of dollars were spent to make computer systems Y2K compliant worldwide. All because the early programmers of the 70's assumed that the software would no longer be relevant or in use after 25 or 30 years. Some transportation systems have lasted a very long time. In Wuppertal, West Germany, a monorail system placed in service in 1902 has been in continuous service ever since as the backbone transport system of the city. Therefore, we simply cannot afford to make the Y2K mistake, and assume that the PRT systems of today's design will not be in use by the time various cities may want to merge their systems. This mistake could also cost billions. Nothing could be more shortsighted.

To establish compatibility standards for PRT, and make them stick, is easier said than done. Every design which has been built and tested so far, or even conceived, consists of the inventor's particular concept. There is nothing remotely resembling unanimity. This was understandable and even laudable when the design was in its infancy, but now that a clear picture has emerged of a modern PRT system embodying all of the desirable feature with none of the drawbacks, it is time to make a bid for uniform standards.

One might hope that the Federal government would be helpful in establishing standards for PRT systems that could apply across the country. Unfortunately, the Federal role in the development of PRT technology has long since become more obstructive than helpful. While the early work was funded with Federal research grants, the first Federal demonstration project (Morgantown) was fatally compromised by electoral politics in the early 1970's. The lobbying of the conventional transit interests has kept PRT off the Federal radar screen ever since. It is unclear whether we can look to the Federal government for any sort of help on PRT in the future.

From time to time, some brave soul in one of the Federal government departments takes it upon himself to inquire regarding the details of PRT. Such departure from the norm represents genuine interest, as well as an attitude to change things, and is deserving of respect and admiration. But whether such individual behavior, almost akin to whistle-blowing, can be effective against the momentum for the status quo within the government remains to be seen.

A further cautionary note is issued by Jerry Kieffer. Great care must be exercised, particularly if any government agency is involved, to insure that standards are not set so broadly as to include all or most proponents of PRT systems, thereby incorporating requirements of much heavier designs. It is a fitting precaution. It would be tragic if the Federal Government, or government at any level, were to mandate that guideways must be at least a certain size or weight, based on the requirements of larger vehicles capable of carrying four or more persons. This would effectively outlaw the slim, lightweight guideways designed for three-person vehicles, thereby eliminating the critical element of optimum PRT design, low weight and low cost. The sought-after standards would have backfired and become a stumbling block. This plea for standardization is rather one of standardization of design, so that ultimately systems can be consolidated and vehicles from different systems can run properly on all guideways.

Chapter 14

The PRT Conferences

The First Conference

It has been stated herein that the proponents of PRT have never had the unanimity of spirit, the political will, or the funds to engage in lobbying activities to any extent. Although this is true, it certainly does not mean that there has been no esprit de corps or loyalty to the cause. While there has been much rivalry, there has also been by a spirit of cooperation. Each developer thought his system had a good chance of being accepted, or he would have stopped working on it; but there was nothing to lose by congeniality.

The evidence of the spirit of sharing and of a cooperative attitude can be seen in a number of areas, but nowhere better than in the successes of the international conferences which were convened for the purpose of promoting advanced transportation ideas.

The first of these international conferences was held in November, 1971, at the Leamington Hotel in Minneapolis. It was not initially intended to be international in scope. Planning a U.S. conference, the committee issued a call for papers, and was inundated with responses. Requests began to come in from outside the U.S. Eventually it became clear that the scope of the conference should be made international. The conference was a resounding success. About 400 people attended from the United States and seven foreign countries. In those early days, ideas of every sort were floated; many of them could not stand up to careful engineering analysis. However, the conference was the first documented indication of how much interest there was worldwide in advanced transportation concepts.

This conference may have been the occasion at which the use of "Personal Rapid Transit" came into general use. The name of the conference had been decided to be "The National Conference on Personal Rapid Transit". The papers which were presented were published in a book, highly sought after, which was named "Personal Rapid Transit". Orders came in from nearly every industrialized country in the world and over three thousand copies were sold.

The conference was very well run. So well, in fact, that it won an award from the Association of University Departments of Conferences, winning out over 200 conferences as the outstanding conference held in 1971 at any university.

The conference was instigated by the University of Minnesota. One of the main purposes of the conference was to consolidate the literature in the field, which had been widely scattered and difficult to obtain.

Subsequent Conferences

The first conference was such a success that ideas for a second conference began to surface, and its promoters began planning for it. The second international conference was held in May, 1973. Planning began a full year in advance with a committee which included members from all over the world. Over 450 persons attended, and more than eighty papers were presented. The resulting book was twice as thick as the first one, further extending the availability of the literature on PRT.

The planners of the first conference had hoped to get a highly-placed representative from UMTA, the Urban Mass Transportation

Authority, as a guest speaker. The organizers had not realized how capricious government agencies can be. PRT was not politically in vogue at that time; not only was a speaker not provided, but also the UMTA administrator, Carlos Villereal, refused to let any of his people attend. To make sure, he scheduled a major conference of his people during the same time. He also transmitted the message to the PRT planners that UMTA's mandate was to back all forms of transportation, and that any conference which specialized only in PRT was not appropriate.

In obtaining a speaker for the second conference, however, they were more successful. Villereal had been replaced by a new administrator, Frank Herringer. There was a new political climate in UMTA, and Herringer himself came to deliver the keynote luncheon address. Several members of the Department of Transportation gave papers. Altogether, the second conference was another tremendous success.

In September, 1975, the third conference was held in Denver. As a result of the Morgantown debacle, Congress had canceled the funds it had allocated to construct a test track in the Denver suburb of Broomfield. Enthusiasm in Denver was at low ebb, and the conference helped to restore confidence in PRT. While the conference was not quite as well attended as the previous ones, overall it was considered a rousing success.

Dr. Jarold A. Kieffer had long been involved in PRT efforts and had been working closely with others in the field. Dr. Kieffer figured prominently in the organizing of all of these international conventions.

At this Denver conference a new organization, the Advanced Transit Association (ATRA), was formed. ATRA was given the role of convening future conferences. As a neutral body, however, its function was to promote all forms of advanced transportation without bias.

Acting in its new responsibility, ATRA convened the fourth international conference on Advanced Transportation. It was held in Indianapolis in 1978. Again, the conference was a great success;

but one participant recalls in his writings that the fledgling ATRA "nearly went broke" mounting this conference. Somehow, one of the functionaries made a serious misjudgement and ordered 15,000 copies of the book which was made up of the papers presented and proceedings. One way or another, ATRA muddled through, and went on to become the nation's only advocate of new transit technology.

The last conference, to date, was held in November of 1996, in Minneapolis. Professor Charles W. Harris of Harvard University was on the planning committee for this conference. Jerry Kieffer again was on the planning committee of this last conference and also played an important role, delivering the kickoff speech on the first morning, entitled "The Fundamental Gap in Urban Transportation". The lead paper, *The Simple, Compelling Case for PRT*, was presented by William A. Wilde, a Senior Project Manager at Carter and Burgess, Inc., Denver, Colorado. Two papers were contributed by Swedish experts Ingmar Andreasson and Elsa Rosenblad from Chalmers University of Technology at Gothenberg, Sweden. The development of the Raytheon PRT system, PRT-2000, was presented by Steven Gluck of Raytheon. Ed Anderson presented a paper on *Control of PRT Systems*. A number of other experts expounded on PRT and on other forms of advanced transportation. This conference topped all previous records for attendance, representation by foreign and domestic contributors, and widespread interest.

Future Conferences

Each of these international conferences contributed greatly to the growing body of knowledge of advanced transportation systems. They were a forum in which ideas of every sort could be advanced. Every proposal no matter how radical received the undivided attention of the participants as the papers were presented. Many different ideas for PRT and for other forms of advanced transportation were offered, but through it all, a consensus of design was slowly developing which embodied the desirable features of PRT and discarded the undesirable ones. This is not to say, however, that radical forms are no longer being promoted. A perusal of the many Web sites for various forms of PRT leaves no doubt that there are still many dissenters and new inventors. But with each conference, the gradually emerging consensus of the optimum PRT design was becoming more evident.

In fact, in this writer's opinion it is questionable whether further conferences, and they are sure to come, will continue to be as valuable as they have been in the past. While they were of inestimable value, they have, in a sense, served their purpose. The main features of PRT have been tacitly approved and fairly well accepted at this point. Further conferences would be rather like preaching to the choir. The conferees are already "saved"; what is needed now is a means to advise the world of the benefits of PRT. It may be true that widespread understanding and acceptance of the transportation renaissance phenomenon will not come about until actual installation has occurred, and people can see and ride on this marvel of technology.

Chapter 15

Which System?

The ULTra System

Although there is a growing worldwide consensus as to what factors constitute the design of the optimum PRT system, there is by no means unanimity on this score. It would seem that inventors of PRT systems are still not immune from the tendency to forge ahead with creation of hardware which will fulfill their particular invention, without studying *all* of the factors with which a complete PRT system must come to grips.

Some of these vary only in certain details, but others are radically different. The latter usually have one thing in common: they are the product of an inventor who is relatively new in the field, and has not been exposed to the accumulated knowledge of over three decades. Those that are radically different characteristically do not stand up to serious engineering scrutiny.

In this age of information technology, some of these ideas are lavishly presented on the inventor's own Web page, where the concepts are glowingly illustrated with style in full color. There is no question that at least some of these, given enough time and money, could be made to work. But they are usually delinquent in meeting one or more aspects of a truly viable PRT system, as delineated in Chapter Two. One could only wish that the engineering was up to the standards of the glowing presentations.

It would seem in some respects that the European PRT

developers are ahead of their U. S. counterparts. Mr. M. V. Lowson in the U. K. and Mr. Palle Jensen in Denmark have developed impressive systems. Both of these developers have already established sources of funding for the eventual implementation of their systems. The U. K. system "ULTra", which stands for Ultra Light Transport, is one which embodies almost all of the design characteristics of good PRT. Building on the previous British design "Cabtrack" as well as the important attributes of good design promulgated at the various international conferences, and with the cooperation of the University of Bristol, the designers have developed a promising design. ULTra incorporates a method for "steering from within the vehicle, rather than by points in the track", which amounts to an onboard switch. The control system does not seem to be firmed up as yet, as it is indicated that this will be completed in the next phase. But ULTra expects to be operational by 2003, and has extensive plans for incorporation of the system in the city of Bristol.

ULTra deviates from optimum design standards in several respects. It postulates a four-person vehicle, which means two rows of seats, with attendant added weight. The guideway design is such that it appears that snow could accumulate, although the inventors state that the system is designed to cope with snow and ice. The design appears to use an automotive-type chassis, which could be subject to derailment and traction problems. Nevertheless, ULTra represents a significant development.

The RUF Design; the Dual Mode Concept

As the science of PRT design has matured, many original ideas have been discarded, and many others have been accepted. One of the first of the early concepts to be challenged by many PRT researchers was the "dual mode" concept, in which vehicles were postulated which would be able to travel on both conventional

roadways and on a PRT guideway. Bill Alden, the originator of the
StaRRcar which eventually became the Morgantown system, was
enamored of this idea at first and had to work his way through it,
eventually abandoning it for the simplicity of the single mode
concept.

Yet the allure of dual mode persists to this day. There are
presently about ten Web sites which promote various kinds of dual
mode systems. There is even a dual mode debate page. This concept
is enticing at first encounter—it seems to alleviate traffic congestion,
provide nonstop travel direct to the destination, and provide safer
automatic control, which, even in Bill Alden's time, was recognized
to provide far safer operation than human judgment. The concept
appears attractive because of the notion that a traveler can move
flexibly from home to street, to guideway, to street and to
destination.

One of these Web sites is the RUF (Rapid, Urban, Flexible)
system, which consists of electric vehicles which can be operated
both on the conventional street system and on a rail facility. Its
inventor, Palle Jensen, a Dane, envisions both public and private
ownership of vehicles which could be driven on regular streets,
then entering the rail system by running on a different set of wheels
for automatic conveyance and control. Jensen proposes a number
of other difficult concepts, including large and small cars and special cars for freight. The system would have the ability to connect
and disconnect these cars into coupled trains automatically. The
Web page is silent regarding a control system for all of this.

Aside from all of the normal arguments against dual mode as
mentioned later, Jensen's weakest link is possibly in connection
with the switching. The cars straddle an A-shaped guideway on
which the cars run on special wheels. Because of this, the cars
have, running lengthwise inside the cabin, a large hump, which
Jensen admits is somewhat of an inconvenience. (Passengers would
be required to be able to access the car from both sides of the track,
which complicates station design.) This guideway has one
admirable characteristic: it cannot collect snow. However, since it

could not be moved physically for switching, Jensen proposes that the guideways terminate at all switches, at which point the cars would run on their street wheels upon a flat surface (which can collect snow) by automatic guidance to the proper new guideway. This concept is fraught with danger because of the possibility of a car's failing while on its street wheels, which in all probability would need to have pneumatic tires, subject to flats. He concedes that the cars would need to slow to half speed at all switching locations. Jensen apparently does not envision the great number of switches or merge and diverge points which are typical on proposed U. S. networks, but perhaps the concept has validity for use in Denmark.

Jensen also suggests flexible fares such as that an entire train of cars would depart at once, rather than waiting, if the fare was high enough. He even suggests a hybrid unit using a gasoline engine which could be mounted in the lengthwise hump in the cars, which would have to be removed quickly when the unit went onto the guideway. Apparently nothing is too complicated for Jensen's fertile imagination. Nevertheless, he vigorously defends his ideas on the dual mode debate page on the Web.

There is no question that Jensen is a dedicated inventor, and that he has quite a following, particularly among the government funding sources in Denmark. He has presented papers at several of the international conferences. He is not a force to be written off spontaneously.

Jensen has been able to obtain funding to promote his work, and in the official opening of the test track on June 9, 2000, the concept was successfully tested with a not very refined car and track, with which it was demonstrated that the car can indeed move off the street wheels and onto the A-shaped track, and back to the street again. Photos illustrating this demonstration are included on the RUF Web page.

However, to many PRT proponents, the dual mode idea has some very serious drawbacks. Every vehicle upon entering the ramp would have to be subjected to extensive checks of the PRT functions of the vehicle, and means would have to be provided for the vehicle to exit if it did not pass. Since the maintenance of the vehicle would not be under the control of the PRT authorities, the verification would have to be very rigorous, as a defective vehicle could jeopardize the entire system. This testing would have to be done automatically, otherwise the time and expense of manual inspection by humans would negate the alleged advantages. There is considerable doubt among PRT authorities that it even would be possible to insure that each vehicle would be absolutely safe to enter the ramp.

Then there is the question of a mechanical breakdown of some sort. This simply cannot be allowed to happen, as a breakdown on the main line would stop all traffic. Even such a simple thing as a flat tire would be catastrophic (Most single mode PRT designs call for cushioned rubber tires which cannot go flat.) The designers of some PRT vehicles have gone to great lengths to insure that a breakdown would be extremely unlikely, and have developed means for dealing with them quickly and safely if they should occur. The breakdown of a modern automobile is far more likely than that of a PRT vehicle.

One of the main advantages of regular (or single mode or captive-vehicle) PRT is that there is no need to park the vehicle when it arrives at its destination. With dual mode, one would have the unpleasant fact that it would be necessary to exit the guideway and park the vehicle in the usual manner (or in some automatic manner as envisioned by dual mode proponents). The space required for parking storage would be the same as for automobiles, because it would be necessary for any vehicle to be available when needed. Storage of single-mode PRT vehicles is vastly simpler. All vehicles can be stored compactly, since only the first in line need be accessible.

Another serious disadvantage of dual mode is that in single mode PRT, no vehicle "belongs" to anyone; all cars are identical, and any car performs equally efficiently for any passenger. To introduce some privately-owned vehicles into the system ushers in complications which would give nightmares to any control system computer expert.

In any dual mode plan, since the vehicle must operate on city streets and highways, it must have all the attributes of an automobile. It must be designed for collisions, and must include a suspension system of springs, shock absorbers, and pneumatic tires for rough roads. This will inevitably increase the weight of the vehicle substantially, negating one of the principle tenants of good PRT design: minimum weight. The cost of the vehicle will also be a great deal more.

Dual mode does nothing for the rapidly growing older population, which has increasing numbers of people who don't drive or fear driving in today's congested traffic conditions. Yet, most of these people want to remain involved in community life but are, in fact, often marooned and needlessly isolated or dependent upon others for transportation.

When the dual mode vehicle leaves the system, it may encounter a traffic-clogged condition in the central city or elsewhere, and be unable to exit. This could cause an unacceptable backup of vehicles, even jeopardizing the flow on the main line.

Finally, the efficient, compact, snow-tolerant guideways of modern PRT design could not be used with dual mode. To accommodate the vehicle, which would have to be much like an automobile in order to travel on streets and highways, the guideway would have to be of U-shaped design, large, unsightly, and heavy. The strategic weight advantage of modern PRT design would be lost, and snow removal or melting problems would be enormous (Palle Jensen's RUF design is a notable exception).

To many developers of PRT technology, the shortcomings of dual mode exclude it from the category of true PRT. To these folks, dual mode has been relegated today to its place in history as an interesting concept, but not practical.

Returning again to the British ULTra concept, the design is stated to be single mode at first, but dual mode is contemplated to be eventually incorporated, as "it is believed to be essential to start and finish the journey at home". With this declaration, the designers are letting themselves in for substantial design headaches. "ULTra" stands for "Ultra Light Transport". If dual mode is to be incorporated, this is a gross contradiction. The guideway will have to be designed at the outset to accommodate the much heavier cars appropriate for road travel, even though this may never occur; it will therefore need to be much larger and more obtrusive visually. All of the other concerns about dual mode apply also. It is difficult to imagine how the operational target date of 2003 for ULTra will be possible if all provisions necessary for the eventual incorporation of dual mode are taken into account.

Suspended Vehicles

Another early idea was the concept of suspending the cars from an overhead guideway. Here again, studies have shown that hanging the cars from the guideway is not so simple as having them run above a guideway track; yet there are a number of such designs being seriously promoted today. The most weighty of the objections centers around the fact that switching is much more difficult when the cars are suspended below the guideway. One method is to move the entire track system, which is not only cumbersome and unsafe, but will not permit the short headways which are an essential part of good PRT design. If the track is not moved, designers are confronted with the problem that a slot must be provided for the member from which the cars hang; this slot will of necessity cut across the tracks at each switch point. Various complicated means have been developed for dealing with this. Ed Haltom's early Monocab had a mechanism to unload the wheels and transfer the weight to other wheels as they passed over the slot in the guideway.

One of these suspended systems, which is documented on the Internet, is Sky Tran, which embodies many of the features of good

PRT design. Their Web site leaves many questions unanswered. It makes no mention of how switching is to be achieved. Loading and unloading seem to be accomplished in separated modules, an unnecessary and costly duplication of facilities. No means of obtaining a ticket is illustrated, and the station facility is a single car length, seemingly designed for the loading of only one car at a time. The advantage of multiple loading berths does not appear to be recognized. The web page system lists six different kinds of public vehicles, including an ambulance. But where the ambulance would come from, and how long it would take, is not revealed. Special cars are provided for the handicapped, so the advantage of instant availability for them is lost. More incomprehensible yet is the proposal that there would be four different kinds of *private* vehicles. How they would be called up, and what one is supposed to do with them after arriving at the destination, is not discussed.

Another serious objection, which applies to all suspended vehicle systems, has to do with the design of the supporting columns. These need to be off-center and much longer then a a simple support column in order to support the guideway from above, and therefore are required to be much stronger and heavier; in fact, they need to be about twice as heavy when wind loads are considered. The foundations for each column therefore also would need to be twice as large. A further objection has to do with the natural frequency of vibration of the guideway. A smoother ride and less stress in the guideway results if the frequency of vibration can be kept high. Dr. Jack Irving, who was largely responsible for the impressive work of The Aerospace Corporation, has shown that clamping the guideway from below as with a car-above-guideway system results in a higher frequency of vibration.

Systems are still being proposed using air suspension and magnetic levitation, although many tests have shown they are not so practical as simple wheels. Quiet operation on smooth cushioned rubber tires is far preferable. However, we may not have heard the last of magnetic suspension for high-speed inter-city advanced transportation, where it remains practical.

One would think that after a few systems which conclusively demonstrated how splendidly a wide, U-shaped guideway could accumulate snow actually had been built, this design would have been scrapped. After all, although not true PRT, the Hovair system of Otis Elevator, installed at Duke University, and the monstrosity at Morgantown had already proved this to perfection. Yet the Raytheon PRT-2000 system, designed and tested in very recent times, had a snow-catching guideway which, in terms of the amount of snow captured, can compete with the best of them.

Accepted Features

But, just as surely as some ideas have proved unworkable, other concepts have become more and more ensconced in the accepted design criteria. Early on, the elevated idea gained ascendancy. The avoidance of collisions with other transportation, and the ability to be erected upon existing rights-of-way were features too important to be ignored.

Automatic control of the vehicles has been a recognized component of design since the inception of PRT, and has become an absolutely vital element as knowledge has accumulated.

The condition that all stations needed to be on separate sidings off the main line was also a key point upon which there was early consensus. True PRT operation would be impossible without it.

By the time the last international conferences were held, it had become clear to most designers that the cars needed to be very small and very light in weight. By giving careful consideration to size and weight, the cost of the system would be such that it would not need to be subsidized, and in fact could earn a profit. The onboard switch was fast becoming accepted as a necessity. Linear electric propulsion was becoming the leading contender for propulsion. The Raytheon PRT-2000 design violated all of these except for the onboard switch.

Taxi 2000

The Taxi 2000 Web site is by far the most comprehensive of any PRT system on the Internet. It provides links to all known PRT and advanced transportation systems, as supplied by the University of Washington, so that it not necessary to leave the Taxi 2000 site to learn about other systems. Whereas many inventors leave some questions unanswered, the Taxi 2000 Web site is remarkably thorough. Among the list of a dozen titles covering all aspects, there is a list of commonly asked questions, with the answers. Every question which has been asked for years is included; there are no questions to which the answer is an embarrassment.

The Taxi 2000 system is the only system that explains how merging is accomplished: by a deceleration or dropping back of vehicles on the main line to *create* an opening for the merging vehicle. (Some systems illustrated on the Internet are silent as to how merging is to be accomplished. Other systems simply provide for a waiting period until a space between cars comes along into which the waiting vehicle can merge.)

There are no unique items that need to be invented specially for the Taxi 2000 PRT application. All of the control and propulsion components are commercially available as "off the shelf" production items, or as modifications which could be readily produced.

Many authorities today recognize the Taxi 2000 system to be the outstanding PRT system. It has won three independent competitions of PRT designs: SeaTac in 1992, the Chicago RTA in 1993, and Forward Quest Cincinnati in 1998. No other system has won any. Proponents of PRT in the Seattle area and elsewhere have selected the design for illustration purposes. The system designed for Korea by Ray MacDonald, as described later, owed much of its specifics to the Taxi 2000 design, and in fact deviated principally only where patent considerations required changing the design.

Optimum Characteristics

The optimum characteristics which should be embodied in a good PRT system may be summarized as follows:

> The compact, lightweight vehicle, running on quiet cushioned rubber tires, seats up to three grown persons on a comfortable bench-type seat. There is ample room for baggage. Each car can accept a wheelchair; thus, every car is a handicap car. Every car has its own dual computers, heating and air conditioning, electrical propulsion and braking by linear induction motors, and a pleasing aerodynamic shape.
>
> The track, called a *guideway,* is elevated normally at a 16-foot clearance above the ground, and supported on columns normally at 60-foot spacing. A guideway design which is snow-tolerant encloses flat steel running surfaces in a square or rectangular shape, having a slot at the top through which the structural members pass that connect the car to the wheels. The wheels include side-mounted wheels that run on vertical surfaces for lateral stability. It is impossible for a vehicle to derail or tip over. The bottom of the guideway enclosure is open, so that snow that enters through the slot falls out harmlessly at the bottom. The guideway can be erected or altered with very little disruption to other transportation or pedestrians.
>
> Every station is on a siding, parallel with the main line, with a switch, called a diverge point, at one end to allow cars to leave the mainline, and a switch, called a merge point, at the other end to regain the main line. No car ever stops on

the main line, only at the stations. Thus, every car can travel directly to its destination station on the main line where the traffic is continuously moving.

The switching mechanism is self-contained *in each car.* There are no moving components in the guideway. Each car is programmed to remain on the main line or switch off, in advance of the diverge point. Thus, no accident can occur due to a switch in the track in the process of throwing as a car passes.

Depending on traffic requirements, stations are designed to have few or many berths, which are separate locations along the guideway station siding at which the cars stop. A passenger can board any available car at any berth, to travel to any station on the system, called the network.

The control system must integrate the movement of every vehicle on the system. Each car receives its coded designation from a ticket purchased by the passenger. The car leaves the station and accelerates up to main line speed. The merging of all vehicles both here and at all other merge points in some designs is handled by wayside computers, until the car is finally diverged off at its destination. The best route on the network is selected by the wayside computers as the vehicle passes each diverge point, thus allowing for possible corrections along the way due, for example, to too heavy a flow on some segment.

Today we stand poised on the threshold, a hairsbreadth away from actual implementation. The first actual installation will set in motion the flowering of the transportation renaissance.

Chapter 16

The Computer Simulations

The Irreplaceable Simulations

The present state of the art of PRT development would not be possible without Dr. Anderson's development of the science of computer simulations. His simulations are a precise duplication of all aspects of a given proposed PRT system. Based upon actual maps of a city's streets, the graphic display shows the entire network of a system in dynamic operation. Any segment can be enlarged and viewed separately. In close-up station view, dots representing people may be seen entering and exiting the cars. In layout view, it may be observed that each car leaving a station does not travel just to the next station; it will pass up many stations with available berths on its way to a definite destination.

At first viewing, the display appears to be a nice exercise in computer display logic, with little dots traveling at uniform speed around various loops, and blending at the merge points, and with no collisions ever occurring at these points. It is apparent that some computer logic has been employed to prevent these collisions from happening. But beyond that, the true complexity is not readily apparent.

In actual fact, thousands of signals are being received and sent every few milliseconds with respect to each car in the system so that its exact speed and position are known within a few millimeters, actual size. The position and speed of each car is adjusted at merge points, so that cars will automatically slip back a small amount to allow space for a car coming from a station to merge. The amount of space on the main line is constantly monitored, and no car is allowed to leave a station until there is an adequate opening for it.

The formidable tasks in generating a simulation of even a small network are exacting. For example, each curve on the system, none of which are simple circle segments, must be entered by means of its mathematical formula. The circular part of the curve is preceded and followed by a transitional section. The complete mathematical expression including these transitions must be entered for each curve at the exact coordinates. When each car enters each curve, it follows the mathematical formula for the curve as it travels around it.

One might ask why it is necessary to go to such extreme lengths. After all, is this not just a nice computer display to illustrate the idea of PRT? The answer is that it is not. Dr. Anderson's computer simulations are not just illustrations; they are complete operating systems capable of operating the actual PRT system which they represent. This may sound exaggerated, but it is literally true. All of the information needed to power up the computers in each car, the wayside computers at switches, and the master computer resides in the memory systems of the computer simulation and can easily be delegated to the respective computers.

Every parameter of the real system must be duplicated. No shortcuts of any kind can be tolerated. Otherwise, over a long period of time, small errors in speed and position may become cumulative, and eventually cars could actually collide. This is why, when the simulation is finally achieved, it has the capability of actually operating a real PRT system.

Dr. Anderson's peers hold that his computer simulations are truly a first in the field of computer science, and, what is more, they have never been duplicated. Without this important breakthrough, the practical utilization of PRT systems would be nearly impossible. The simulations are an indispensable tool in analyzing proposed systems and in energizing the actual operating components.

The examples given in the chapter titled *The Downsides* serve to show how very rigorous and complete Dr. Anderson's calculations and computer simulations really are, when it is realized that even the minor annoyances of a wave-off or a short wait are so thoroughly examined and dealt with. His computer simulations fully incorporate the possibilities of a wave-off or a shortage of vehicles at any given station.

It the 1970's, conventional wisdom declared that the operation of PRT systems would require huge computers. The fact is that a typical Taxi 2000 simulation of a proposed installation, which contains *all* of the data necessary to actually operate the system, occupies only about one five thousandths of the memory of a typical laptop computer.

Dr. Anderson's computer acumen notwithstanding, it is true that the Taxi 2000 simulations would not be what they are today were it not for the outstanding contribution of John Braff, the Vice President for Computer Technology for Taxi 2000. Braff has significantly augmented and, in some instances, equaled even Anderson's formidable talents. Furthermore, he has accomplished substantial achievements in helping to insure the security of the codes on which the Taxi 2000 simulations are based. These simulations cannot be reverse-engineered in order to achieve the original definitive code.

Chapter 17

The Disadvantaged

Full Service to All

The needs of handicapped persons were not of primary concern to the early inventors. This is still true of some of the systems being proposed today. Many inventors forged ahead with their individual concept of PRT, intent more upon proving that it was feasible than with addressing peripheral considerations. Some of their ideas showed some signs of feasibility, but their systems proved to be unmarketable because of some shortcoming or other.

In modern PRT design, one of the goals is that the system not discriminate in any way against any handicapped person. This includes the blind, deaf, dumb, or immobile. Another goal is to make the system easy and safe for children to use.

The fact that there are no humans to deal with at a typical PRT station is in reality an advantage to the handicapped. Thus, a person who is deaf does not need to be able to hear what a ticket seller would say to him. A person who is unable to speak does not need to talk with anyone to buy his ticket or board the vehicle.

In bus terminals or train stations, departing buses or trains are often announced on the loudspeaker, a distinct disadvantage to someone who is deaf or somewhat hearing-impaired. Given the poor quality of the PA systems and the reverberation of the buildings, such messages are hard enough to decipher even with normal hearing. Often it is necessary to ask questions in order to find the right bus or the right train on the proper track, a real problem for someone who cannot speak or hear. PRT eliminates these problems.

People who are blind can accomplish things that seem pretty amazing to those of us with normal vision. They board buses, go downtown, cross busy thoroughfares, go shopping. The challenge to PRT designers will be to make buying a ticket and boarding a vehicle no more daunting than these other accomplishments.

Buying a ticket on a small system of only a few stations, as the first installations are expected to be, should not be too difficult for the blind. The stations can be identified by braille, and the receptor for the dollar bills or the card can have tapered entree for easy insertion. In the case of a large system with perhaps 100 stations, it may be necessary for the sightless to ask assistance of some other passenger. Although human nature has some deplorable characteristics, very few people would refuse to give the few seconds required for such help.

With ticket in hand, a blind person should encounter no further problem. Braille-like embossed bumps on the ticket will advise which end and which side up should be inserted into the ticket slot. With a cane, a blind person can tell easily if there is a car in the berth, ready for him.

One of the reasons that earlier designers, and some people yet today, opted for vehicles of four or more people was that it would be more pleasant for families of more than three to be able to travel together. This is an insidious argument and one which seems very plausible at first blush. But accommodating more than three raises very serious problems.

Designing PRT vehicles is a little like designing airplanes. Every pound counts. Whatever can be done to keep the vehicle weight to a minimum is critical, because this vitally affects the size and cost of the guideway. Since thousands of miles of guideways will need to be built, the cost of the entire system is greatly affected by the size and weight of the vehicles. When applied to the number of passengers, it is clear that one, two, or three people can be accommodated nicely on a bench-type seat. But four adults would require two rows of seating, whether bench-type or bucket seats. This would affect the length and weight of the car to a marked degree; all the car's requirements such as propulsion, braking, heating and air conditioning would need to be larger. Headways and berthing spaces would have to be longer, therefore stations also would have to be longer. The largest expense of all would be in the beefed-up guideway which would be required for the heavier cars.

The bench-type seats can, however, accommodate an adult and several small children. While it would be nice if entire families could travel together, the trade-off is simply not worth it. Children can easily take the next car, travel in complete safety, and arrive at the destination directly after their parents. Or, the parents can split up, each traveling with some of the children.

Accommodation of wheelchairs has been incorporated in all recent PRT designs, such as the Raytheon PRT-2000 and Ray MacDonald's design, *PRT Korea*, for Woo-Bo Enterprises of Korea. While some designers toyed with (and are still promoting in current designs) the idea of having a few special cars available which could take wheelchairs, most designers long ago realized that every car should be a wheelchair car, and this thinking has pervaded the current design logic.

However, there is one caveat too important to be ignored. Raytheon was persuaded by the Chicago RTA to ignore it, with tragic results. That caveat is that the proper disposition of the wheelchair is facing sideways within the vehicle. In the case of Raytheon, the RTA people, with the help of transportation "experts", actually a handicapped committee uninformed about the consequences, insisted that the wheelchair face forward in the car. This resulted in the car's length being increased by over three feet, a gigantic leap in car size and weight. The resulting increase in expense of all system components was so drastic that Raytheon has never found a buyer for its product.

It certainly can be expected that all facilitators, as the term is used in the last chapter herein, will give attention to the needs of handicapped persons. One way or another, every PRT system of any standing makes provision for the conveyance of the disadvantaged.

Chapter 18

The Objections

Common Misconceptions

Any new idea or development runs into a host of detractors. PRT is no exception. It is claimed to be unsightly, expensive, isolating, unproven, unsafe, intimidating, inefficient. All of the above objections are spurious and untrue and are easily refuted by an investigation of the facts, as established by the descriptions of PRT in the foregoing chapters. But there are other more serious ones, which, although they contain fundamental errors in reasoning, are not so easy to dispel.

One of these is the conviction, easy enough to identify with upon first thought, that a PRT system would never be able to keep up with the huge crowds exiting from a sporting event or other happenings involving thousands of people. Before analyzing this, it is good to think of how well existing forms of transportation perform. Perhaps almost all of us have had the trying experience of waiting endlessly in a parking lot or ramp after a game while hundreds of cars queue up for the one-at-a-time exit, onto a street which is already choked with traffic. Or heading for the busses, finding the right bus, waiting until the passenger count is complete or the bus is filled, and then jockeying for position to exit onto that crowded thoroughfare. PRT does not have to perform very well at all to exceed these examples.

In fact, PRT does perform very well. The stations serving a

sports stadium would be some of the largest on the network. As mentioned, the communities of Cincinnati, Covington, and New-port have taken the first steps toward the implementation of PRT. The facilities tentatively designed for the home of the Cincinnati Reds will consist of four stations, each having 14 berths. Crowds do not discharge simultaneously at an event. People arrive in small groups separated by at least several seconds. The time needed to load a car and depart is only in the nature of several seconds. With cars departing every few seconds and empty cars arriving continu-ously, the boarding process goes on continuously. Extensive calcu-lations have shown that this process proceeds quite smoothly. In the computer simulation developed for Cincinnati and environs, the average wait time at the peak traffic after a game is less than one minute. Even under the most extreme conditions the waiting time very seldom would exceed three minutes. Once on the net-work, there would be no congestion; movement is continuous on the main line. Compare this with the half-hour or more which is often typical of conventional transportation before the stadium is left behind.

Some critics, with ill-disguised contempt, declare that it is ridiculous to imagine that cars holding only three people could equal buses holding forty people or trains holding hundreds, and, furthermore, that the cost of such vehicles must be exorbitant. Such detractors simply have not done their mathematics. The time used to load a string of empty vehicles waiting in their berths is less than that typically required to load a bus. PRT passengers load in parallel, rather than in series through one door as in a bus, making loading much faster. The transit time for a bus is also far greater, stopping as it must for every red traffic light and every passenger getting on or off.

It is no doubt true that the first few PRT vehicles to be built will be expensive. Economies of scale and of identical replication will soon bring these costs down. Because of this, the cost of vehicles for even the first PRT system are expected to be reasonable. When photo-voltaic cells were first invented, scoffers said that it was a nice laboratory device, but too expensive to ever be useful. But as mass production techniques and new methods have been introduced, the cost has come down steadily until today photovoltaic cells find many applications where utility power is not available. The same price effect is true of computers and many other items.

Some faultfinders have attempted to make a case that PRT would not serve neighborhoods well, because the lines would be too far apart; they assert that light rail would be a far better choice. Such critics do not understand the fundamental difference of PRT. Study after study of both proposed and existing light rail has shown that light rail is only practical where extremely high population density exists along the light rail corridor. Very few cities meet this requirement. PRT, on the other hand, can be built quite economically to *cover* a neighborhood. A PRT network can consist of a series of loops in which the guideways are, say, no more than one-half mile apart, with stations at half-mile intervals. Thus the farthest any passenger would have to walk to board the system would be one-quarter mile. Most passengers would walk less than that.

This is not to say that all PRT systems will be built in this fashion. It is far more likely, particularly in the early installations, that systems will be built which will handle the greatest need for transportation in areas of high congestion, and between points most frequented by passengers. Thus, for example, the Sky Loop, the name given the system under extensive investigation and planning by the cities of Cincinnati, Covington, and Newport, will link these communities and their major attractions and facilities on both sides of the Ohio river, providing for greatly enhanced economic opportunities as well as resolving serious congestion and parking problems.

Professor Vukan Vuchic

Vukan Vuchic, Professor of Transportation Engineering at the University of Pennsylvania, is an outspoken critic of PRT. His writings run the full gamut of objections, from the small size of cars (he feels they are inferior because they can carry only a small fraction of that of a bus or train) to the fact that in three decades since the idea of PRT surfaced, there has never been an actual installation (which Professor Vuchic feels demonstrates that it must have serious shortcomings).

Professor Vuchic's conclusions are called into question by some because he does not put any numbers to the claims he makes. Thus, he asserts that "a systematic technical analysis shows a far less favorable picture" than that posed by the promoters. But it hard to see how a "systematic technical analysis" can be made without producing any numerical values, or referring to any studies in which ridership, costs, headway (time between cars) or in fact any other element are documented by tallying numbers of riders, dollar values, or distance or time values, respectively. Various studies which have been done, for example, the Barton-Aschman, Inc. study in 1978 made for the city of Indianapolis, found that in comparing a range of vehicle sizes from 100 person capacity to 3 person capacity, the smaller the vehicle, the lower was the cost per passenger-mile. This was an independent study, which was not particularly promoting PRT.

Professor Vuchic apparently makes his claims on the basis of what seems reasonable. But this type of thinking can lead one far astray in short order. Because it is an entirely new discipline, conventional wisdom with respect to PRT often can be incorrect. For example, only a very few people would guess that a typical single-track PRT system of modern design can carry 5000 people per hour, as many people as a three-lane freeway filled to capacity. Yet when the numbers are applied, the truth is evident. It has to do with the fact that PRT vehicles all moving at exactly the same speed can be as close as only a few feet, following each other at headways as short as one-half second, yet in complete safety.

Professor Vuchic makes the assertion that the large investment costs for the sophisticated automation required would be suitable only for large capacity vehicles. The fact is that the fault-tolerant, redundant computers required in each vehicle are now available, off-the-shelf, at surprisingly low prices, which will be even lower when they are ordered by the thousands. The same is true of the wayside computers required at each merge and diverge point.

Professor Vuchic says that the slowdown of traffic on the freeways at peak hours illustrates that small vehicles are not suitable for high passenger volumes. What it really illustrates is that the freeways are grossly overloaded at such times and are forced to handle more traffic than they were designed for, as any knowledgeable traffic engineer will agree.

One issue that Professor Vuchic raises is the question of how acceptable the elevated guideways will be in residential areas. Vuchic asserts that "the environmental impact of the guideways would be unacceptable." There is no doubt but that this may be a problem in some cases, and possibly some people will put up quite a fuss. But many others regard the guideways and small cars as evidence of progress, and even sculptural in quality. Vuchic says the issue is so important that there are *no* applications where PRT would be practical, and that it makes many other problems with PRT irrelevant. "A few of them are worth mentioning," he says, "to further illustrate the impracticability of the concept."

One of these he claims is that PRT systems will always require a large number of vehicles cruising empty; "an expensive operation". He does not address the fact that buses and trains run empty most of the time. With a typical one third of the cars empty, PRT still would have a better empty ratio than conventional transportation.

Professor Vuchic claims that the PRT concept has been rejected as unrealistic during the last three decades by dozens of cities in North America, Europe and Japan. He does not recognize that the modern version of PRT has really evolved into its present form only in the last decade or so. And the so-called rejections have resulted more from the caprices of human nature, such as envy, greed, incompetence and timidity than from any deficiency in the capability of PRT. Well-documented cases in many references testify to this fact. Vuchic does not mention that railroad and other vested interests effectively lobbied PRT out of consideration, and are still doing so today.

Professor Vuchic further asserts that the smaller and cheaper cars and stations of PRT will never compensate for the cost difference of an automatic guided transit (AGT) system like Morgantown. Here again, he uses no figures with which to document his assertion. The figures seem to indicate otherwise. The Morgantown fiasco was one of the largest cost overruns in the history of transportation. This was the major reason it was so lampooned in the press. The costs of a modern PRT system are so far below that of Morgantown that there is no comparison.

Roxanne Warren, Author

Roxanne Warren, the author of *The Urban Oasis*, is another critic of personal rapid transit. Her criticism is based not so much on her perceived shortcomings of PRT as upon her conviction that it would become largely unnecessary under the social organization which she envisions. She is one of a number of planners who has fallen under the spell of the idea of small, organized, functional communities which would be almost entirely self-sufficient. These clusters of population would be planned for the maximum efficient utilization of space, rather than the indiscriminate and wasteful use of space which presently occurs. Ms. Warren is an urban planner, and, among other things, serves on the board of ATRA, the Advanced Transit Authority. Thus she is a position to know that rail transportation can be effective only if there is high density of population along the corridor it serves. The dense living clusters or modules envisioned by Ms. Warren would accomplish this. People could easily walk or bicycle to the rail station. Thus the idea would combat urban sprawl, eliminate the gobbling up of rural space for more and more freeways, reduce pollution (there would be less need for automobiles), and foster social interaction and community spirit.

It's a lovely idea, and one which has been written about extensively by planners and thinkers on many levels. The problem is, it won't work. It could only be implemented in a totalitarian society where people are not free to make economic and personal choices of their own.

In a pleasant rural setting near Minneapolis, a planned community something of this sort was launched. It was funded by private philanthropic money, and was highly touted in the news media as the model of the future. The community, named Jonathan, was planned to be largely self-sufficient. There were to be homes, shopping centers, manufacturing and other businesses, service jobs, recreational facilities including a golf course, in fact, nearly every amenity and requirement one could imagine. It was too large a development to warrant no automobiles, but the road system was local and traffic planning was not a problem.

Jonathan started off well enough. Progress was not as fast as was anticipated, but a number of homes were built of varying tastes and price levels. Owners were allowed to build pretty much what they wanted. The residential portions of Jonathan are as nice as any other typical community. A number of business of different kinds were persuaded to come to Jonathan; over a dozen names start with the word Jonathan. Careful zoning was utilized, and the businesses were well-located and landscaped. The golf course was built, and is as good or better than many of the areas' courses. As a suburban development, Jonathan could be considered a success, in fact, it is considered a nicer place to live or work than many other suburbs. But, as a model for a self-contained functional module, it was not successful.

Most of the people who live in Jonathan work elsewhere. The

employment opportunities in the entire Twin Cities metropolitan area are available to them. Those who do work in Jonathan mostly live elsewhere. In both cases, Jonathan can be easily reached from many suburbs and even Minneapolis. The fact is, most people would rather put up with a considerable amount of driving time in exchange for what they consider a better job or the opportunity to stay in the place where they now live. Similarly, the golf course is frequented by customers from all over the western suburbs of the Twin Cities.

The evidence for this behavior was plain enough to any observer before Jonathan was built, or *The Urban Oasis* was written. People willingly drive in from many nearby towns within 30 or 40 miles to jobs in the Twin Cities. What Jonathan proved is that, in a society where people are free to make their own choices as to where they will live and work, the self-contained functional module is an illusion. The only way it could be workable would be to build it about 200 miles from any other city or town, in which case it is highly questionable whether or not anyone would move there in the first place.

There is nothing objectionable about planned communities. But focusing on them totally neglects meeting the transportation needs of the much vaster and more populous older core areas and older suburban areas. Putting attention on planned communities solely does nothing for overall traffic congestion.

Roxanne Warren does have some unkind (and incorrect) things to say about personal rapid transit. This is all the more surprising since she serves on the Board of Directors of ATRA, an organization which for many years has publicly recognized the clear superiority of PRT over other forms of advanced transportation. Among other things, she claims that PRT will promote urban sprawl. This is simply at variance with the facts. PRT will never be built out into the countryside, enticing people to engage in more urban sprawl. It will be built within city centers, and from city centers into the neighborhoods and suburbs. She and others feel that PRT may force isolation upon us, shut up in our individual vehicles, to the detriment of community discourse and spirit. But how is that any different than our automobiles, in which the ridership during rush hour is less than 1.1 persons per car? And how much discourse is observed on buses and subways? People rarely talk; they are simply concerned with getting to their job or destination, not with engaging in social discourse.

There are many questions in regard to PRT, and every objection must be carefully examined and the necessary corrections made in the design where they are valid. But nothing basically new has turned up to challenge good PRT design in many years. The truth is that almost all first opinions about PRT are hastily-made gut reactions that have no basis in fact. Under careful scrutiny, the objections to PRT fade into insignificance.

Chapter 19

A Major Player

A Lifetime in Transportation

One of the best designers ever to be occupied with PRT development is an engineer named Ray MacDonald. Like Dr. J. Edward Anderson, he has been engaged in proposed PRT systems over much of his lifetime. He has been involved together with Anderson for many years. Anderson calls him "the world's best transportation engineer."

A complete Curriculum Vitae of MacDonald's illustrious history would be beyond the scope of this book, but as early as 1961-1964, when he worked for Christiani & Nielsen in England, he was already chief engineer on construction of M2 Motorway bridges. His comprehensive transportation experience included Montreal Expo '67 Monorail, Embarcadero station design on San Francisco BART system, Sao Paulo Metro station & tunnel design in Brazil, Pearl Ridge Automated People Mover in Hawaii and Honolulu Rapid Transit System planning, Denver PRT Project planning & design, Rio de Janeiro Metro design in Brazil, Indianapolis DPM (Downtown People Mover) Study, Eurotunnel Design Review, Taiwan Metro design, Korean High Speed Railway feasibility study and design, and Bangkok Metro design & construction supervision. His work took him into design of increasingly complex automated transportation systems. Many of these were conceptual, but some were actually built, for example, the

Pearl Ridge people mover, a fully automated system in Honolulu linking two shopping centers, using Rohr Monocab equipment on an aerial guideway.

Ray learned about PRT in an interesting manner. He was asked by his boss to write a paper that would destroy PRT as competition. In late 1971 he was working for Johnson and Mendenhall (DMJM) on a Los Angeles subway project. At that time Aerospace Corporation had completed their initial PRT research work and were pressing the Los Angeles City Government to adopt PRT as their future transport system. The concern of DMJM was that the publicity on the Aerospace Corporation's PRT system might derail their plans. Ray, in his methodical way, called Jack Irving and said that he wanted to be briefed on their PRT system. Jack and his deputy, Harry Bernstein, came over to DMJM and briefed Ray in detail, taking several days to to give Ray a full understanding of PRT. By the end of the briefing, Ray was convinced that this was the best thing he had ever seen in the urban transport field and he instantly became a strong advocate of PRT. However, the pressure from consultants and contractors to promote the LA Metro proved too strong for Aerospace to overcome so an early opportunity was missed.

The Pair in Action

The earliest association of Ed Anderson and Ray MacDonald was in 1974 while working for the Colorado Regional Transportation District (RTD) on the largest study of transit alternatives ever undertaken up to that time. Anderson was assigned to help supervise the work on ridership analysis, which put him in daily contact with some of the best professionals in the U. S. in this field and provided essential background for understanding the problem of ridership analysis. Among other things, he worked with Ray MacDonald on a one-way vs. two-way guideway committee. Although the RTD had sold the public a PRT concept for which they voted positively, under the heavy hand of UMTA the RTD soon demanded that PRT be dropped from consideration in that study. This eliminated all viable options for Denver's low-density urban area and the project terminated ignominiously with a recommendation for a Light Rail Transit system (LRT).

In the fall of 1980 the pair formed Anderson MacDonald, Inc. The purpose of this corporation was to advise the State of Indiana on developing automatic guideway transit (AGT) for the city of Indianapolis. The term AGT was used to encompass all kinds of automated guideway transit. AGT was divided into Shuttle-Loop Transit, Group Rapid Transit, and Personal Rapid Transit. This series of definitions was first clearly spelled out in an OTA (Office of Technical Assessment) study in 1975 in the early days when the salient requirements of PRT were beginning to come into clear focus. The city wanted to explore the whole range of vehicle sizes.

This was one of the first serious studies undertaken for a large city, and the State Assembly had appropriated $300,000 for the purpose. Anderson MacDonald, Inc. contracted with the State of Indiana to supervise Barton Aschman, Inc., a consulting firm, which made a comprehensive study of AGT vehicles using 100, 60, 40, 20, 12, and 3 passengers per vehicle. It is important to note that this was an independent study, not one particularly promoting PRT. Not surprising to Anderson and MacDonald, it was found that the smaller the vehicle, the lower was the cost per passenger mile. This seems to run counter intuitively to what one would think. A small car holding only three people must duplicate all the functions of propulsion, braking, control, air conditioning, and heating of a 12-person car; how could such cars cost less than one-fourth the cost of a 12-person car? The answer lies in the fact that Barton-Aschman were studying the costs of the *whole system*. A guideway capable of supporting 12-passenger cars at short headways has to be many times sturdier than one for 3-passenger cars, and many miles of guideway are required. The columns and

their footings, as well as the amount of land required is also substantially larger. Because of the much higher guideway cost, the
12-passenger system turns out to be more expensive, even though
only one-fourth as many cars are needed. At the other extreme,
that is, the 100-passenger vehicles, the difference is even more
extreme. Now we are talking about trains, and the expense of the
dedicated miles of right-of-way, tracks, roadbed, and the cost of
the rolling stock and equipment puts this alternative into the highest
cost per passenger-mile. Most of the technologies considered were
automated such as the people movers in the Atlanta, Orlando, Tampa,
and Miami airports; however, light rail was also included in the study.

The results of this study, and others like it confirming that
PRT was much more financially viable than other public transport
modes, were revolutionary. But they have yet to be accepted by
most transportation engineers, who are still promoting the vested
interests of consultants, contractors and politicians in the financially
nonviable systems of the past century.

Although the studies achieved a milestone in PRT progress,
the city of Indianapolis did not pursue the implementation of any
AGT system, despite the efforts of Anderson and MacDonald. The
best system around at that time, perhaps the only viable system,
was the German Cabintaxi, but support for an installation of that
system in Hamburg was abruptly canceled by the German
government in 1982.

The German companies DEMAG and MBB were willing to
work a deal to build a system in Indianapolis. The problem was
that Ray and Ed had accepted Cabintaxi with the reservations that
(1) the control system would have to be changed from analog to
digital, (2) the boxy vehicles would have to be redesigned, (3) the
over-under guideway was unnecessarily bulkier than desirable, and
(4) the switch sections of the box beam guideway were unduly
complicated and consequently very expensive.

But even if Cabintaxi could have been made available,
Anderson-MacDonald knew that a better control system would
be needed. The switching means also left much to be desired. Ray

MacDonald undertook an engineering study of the Cabintaxi switching system, which included the guideway design. He obtained quotes from a local steel fabricator, and found that both the guideway and the complete switching mechanism were prohibitively expensive.

Anderson and MacDonald, therefore, turned their attention to the problem of developing a better system. Anderson, then a professor at the University of Minnesota, recruited the help of Mechanical Engineering seniors in developing designs as part of their training by assigning the problem to his senior mechanical engineering design class. He states that the fall quarter class of 1981 contributed a wide range of designs and useful information, but nothing that was really satisfactory. Ed Anderson went on from that point to develop his unique guideway and switch designs which had not been previously patented and, therefore, constituted new state of the art.

The Barton-Aschman study confirmed for the Indianapolis proponents that PRT was viable. Ed Anderson had been working with the Indiana state legislature member Ned Lambkin, Majority Leader of the House, and Dick Doyle, another member of the Indiana Assembly, during most of the seventies. In January of 1983, negotiations were undertaken to jointly form a company. Unfortunately, this was about the same time that the first Minnesota company, Automated Transit Systems, was being formed with the University of Minnesota to develop commercially the patents which had been granted to Ed Anderson. The principals of this company, Roger Staehle, Tony Patami, and Joe Schuster were deeply involved with Ed, and felt that the fledgling company should move slowly and cautiously at first. Because of their long exposure to PRT, the Indiana people were far ahead of them in their appreciation of PRT, and were pushing hard for rapid progress. Thus there was a difference in thinking which caused the proposed deal to fall apart. After having been denied the use of the Cabintaxi system and rebuffed by the new Minnesota corporation, the Indianapolis interest quickly faded into history.

Automated Transit Systems, Inc. had its ups and downs, as described in the chapter entitled *Taxi 2000 and its Predecessor*. Ray MacDonald spent a year with ATS in 1985 as Vice President for Marketing, working for six months in Chicago and six months in Minneapolis. One day he read an article in a Chicago newspaper about a sculptor named John David Mooney. He was an unusual sculptor, and created works of unusual scope, some involving vast lighting arrangements and other effects. But he was more than a sculptor. He was a visionary. Some of this must have become apparent in the article, because MacDonald felt that he must meet the man. He did, and presented the concept of PRT. Mooney almost instantly saw the potential, and, from that time forward, was an avid enthusiast. In his role as one of the major artists in Chicago, he was able to set up meetings with various Chicago officials at which Ed and Ray presented PRT. No one bit, but Mooney did not give up. Four years later, in March of 1989, Mooney had lunch with Thomas J. Riley, a businessman who seemed to have had the ear of all the important people in Chicago. Mooney called Ed right after that lunch to urge that he call Riley, because Riley had gotten excited from Money's description of the Taxi 2000 system. Riley said that the leadership of the Northern Illinois Regional Transportation Authority (RTA), (Gayle Franzen, the new Chairman, and Sam Skinner, former Chairman and just appointed Secretary of Transportion by President Bush) said that they knew that they could not solve the transportation problems in Chicago with just more highways and more conventional rail systems, and felt that their must be a rocket scientist out there somewhere with a usable new idea. Riley was very impressed, and set up a meeting for himself and Gayle Franzen with Ed Anderson and his associate, Dick Daly. This was the breakthrough the PRT boys had been waiting for (it is described in chapter entitled *Raytheon*) leading ultimately to the involvement of Raytheon and the development and testing of Raytheon's system for the RTA.

PRT for Korea

Since the Korean War, the capital city of Seoul has virtually erupted in growth. Every aspect of the economy has mushroomed at an astounding pace, including a veritable explosion in the number of automobiles. Although Seoul was rebuilt with boulevards 14 lanes wide, the side streets are no bigger than they ever were. Consequently, the traffic problems in Seoul are as bad as anywhere in the world. Cars move at a snail's pace. It can take an hour or more to go even a few miles. Parking is horrendous. The city planners were very much aware that something had to be done, but they didn't know what. The Korean Department of Transportation was interested in building new transportation, but thought that light rail offered the best solution.

Ray had gone to Korea in 1983 to work for Louis Berger International on the Seoul to Pusan High Speed Railway Project. Always dedicated to personal rapid transit, Ray gradually worked to convince Kim In Ki, the Chairman of Woo-Bo Engineering Company, the Korean partner of Louis Berger International, that he should invest in PRT. The Korean government was lukewarm; some of its advisors had received their Ph.D.'s under professor Vukan Vuchic of the University of Pennsylvania, one of the leading detractors of PRT. These disciples were effective in cooling the interest of the Korean Department of Transportation in PRT.

The significance of Korea as a potential market for the manufacture and sale of PRT is that Korea has many densely populated cities in which the creation of additional suburbs is prohibited. Korea has additionally developed the industrial capability in electronics, steel and automobile production to provide the capability for PRT manufacturing. Realizing this, even without the endorsement of the Korean Department of Transportation, Woo-Bo Enterprises forged ahead. Kim In Ki had become very enthusiastic. He visited Ed Anderson several times while the latter was at Boston University. Anderson went to

Korea for one week in July 1985 and for two weeks in February, 1996.

In 1990, Ray MacDonald returned to Seoul to manage the Preliminary Engineering on the High Speed Railway Project as Project Engineer. But his efforts on behalf of PRT came to fruition. Kim In Ki decided that Woo-bo should develop a PRT initiative. Working with Woo-Bo as their Project Engineer, and having kept abreast of developments, MacDonald was able to specify the basic design parameters for PRT Korea including the design of the vehicles and guideway. He adhered to the characteristics of good modern PRT design as distilled through the many international conferences and the growing knowledge of proper design.

MacDonald wore several hats besides that of an engineer. He was instrumental in accomplishing much of the preliminary work such as public relations, which needs to be done before a project like PRT can gain acceptance. Financial and technical feasibility studies were prepared for over 15 urban PRT systems. A beautiful, four-color brochure was produced. An excellent video, perhaps the finest one extant, was developed in which the animated PRT system was realistically superimposed in proper scale over actual scenes of roads and proposed rights-of-way. These scenes are among the best in existence, a virtual reality video which realistically illustrates the proposed PRT system skimming merrily over the traffic-clogged streets. Enthusiasm was running high by 1997.

But, suddenly, hopes were dashed to pieces. The Asian monetary crisis, which hit like a hurricane, engulfed Korea as much if not more than any other country. Woo-Bo Enterprises was overextended and found itself near bankruptcy. It became engaged in a desperate struggle for survival and could not even consider any new ventures, let alone pursuing such future uncertainties as PRT.

The intervention of the International Monetary Fund came just in time to rescue Korea from complete and total national insolvency and the anarchy which might have then ensued. But it came at a terrible price. Korea, as well as most other Asian countries, had been acting as if there were no tomorrow. Their fragile economies had never weathered the storm of even a recession; yet this was a depression of the greatest severity. The International Monetary Fund required as a condition of its participation the most austere of measures. All programs which were not absolutely necessary for the operation of the economy of the country had to be eliminated. This, of course, included all future projects like PRT.

For Ray MacDonald, the blow must have come as one of the more unkind cuts in his experience. He had to go from being the most highly respected authority and counselor in his field in the whole country to someone working again in the conventional transportation field. Ray MacDonald had done heroic work in Korea, but the realization of his dream was not to be.

A competent transportation engineer like Ray MacDonald who has worked on many transportation projects besides PRT can survive the change (he shortly found work in a project in Thailand), but it is difficult to predict how long it will take for Korea to regain its footing. Whether Korea will once again take up its position as a leader in the potential implementation of PRT cannot be foretold. But there are encouraging signs. Mr. Kim In Ki still remains enthusiastic, and, in fact, again visited Ed Anderson in Minneapolis as recently as October, 1999, just before the collapse of Raytheon stock prices. Dr. Anderson also received an inquiry from a professor of Electrical Engineering at POSTECH University in Seoul indicating continued interest.

Since his work on PRT Korea for Woo-Bo had to circumvent the Taxi 2000 patents which had been assigned to Raytheon, Ray MacDonald had to come up with some designs which were very innovative. It is true that there is much information in the literature. The international conventions and, in fact, the nature of Dr. Anderson himself as a professor, have been one of the sharing of information toward realizing the eventual crystallization of the defining aspects of good PRT design. Even so, it is a credit to MacDonald's inventive genius that he was able to do this. They included the development of patents for electromagnetic switching, a bar-code navigation system, an electromechanical braking system and integrated structural guideway running surfaces. However, maintaining the basic concept of PRT developed by Taxi 2000 proved to be essential to a financially viable system.

In the area of the control system and related software it was MacDonald's intention to contract with Taxi 2000 for the use of its control system. It was principally for this reason that Kim In Ki came to Minneapolis to visit Taxi 2000 in October of 1999. Dr. Anderson, together with John Braff, Vice President for Computer Technology at Taxi 2000, has devoted countless hours to the perfection of this technology, which is today recognized by their peers as an outstanding achievement. Any equal of the secured codes of Taxi 2000 Corporation is unknown and considered highly unlikely.

Ray MacDonald is to be saluted for his outstanding work on PRT for the Republic of Korea. It may well be at some future date that he will be one of the facilitators described in the final chapter of this book. If so, his participation should be welcomed. There will be plenty of work to go around.

Chapter 20

The Guiding Light

The Prodder

Dr. Jarold (Jerry) Kieffer enjoyed a contributory and prestigious role in the development of our country's affairs. After military service in World War II, he received his Ph.D. in Political Science in 1950 from the University of Minnesota. His career led him into fascinating work in government, research, and teaching. Early in his career he served under President Eisenhower who in 1953 created a three-man committee, consisting of Nelson Rockefeller, Milton Eisenhower, and Arthur Flemming, to advise on key organizational problems in transportation. Kieffer was, first, Flemming's assistant, then, later, Rockefeller's assistant until the latter left to become Governor of New York in 1959. Kieffer states that the intensive work done by this committee eventually led to the creation of the Department of Transportation under the Johnson Administration in the 1960's.

In other roles, during and after these early years, Kieffer served as executive officer to the Secretary of Health, Education, and Welfare and later as chief of program evaluation for that federal department. In 1952-53, he served as Acting Executive Secretary of President Truman's Cabinet Committee on Defense Transportation during the Korean War. He also served as Secretary of the National Cultural Center (1959-1963) and then as its executive director (1961-1963). In these roles, he was responsible for all

planning and other activities for this project that, in 1964, was
renamed the John F. Kennedy Center for the Performing Arts, the
nation's living memorial to the slain president.

Backing into PRT

Jarold Kieffer has been one of the most active in conceptualizing
the practical aspects of PRT with respect to service and cost values.
After leaving federal service in late 1963, Kieffer next became
involved at the state level where he served as executive officer to the
president of the University of Oregon and as a political science
professor. His first inkling of the potential of PRT came as a result
of this tenure, but it did not happen for some time. At first he
championed the need for a high-speed rail system to connect three
universities and a number of four-year colleges spread along the
110-mile Willamette corridor between Eugene and Portland. In
1967, he was chosen to head the development and public policy
administration division of the School of Community Service and
Public Affairs at the University of Oregon. His widely reported
plan for the "Northwest Express" attracted the attention of U. S.
Senator Warren Magnuson, as well as both of the governors of
Oregon and Washington. Magnuson was chairman of the U.S.
Senate's Committee on Interstate and Foreign Commerce, and
brought Kieffer back to Washington to direct development of
legislation that would provide 90 percent federal matching grants
to states, to create planning districts to enhance transportation
linkages. Unfortunately, Senator Magnuson moved on to other
responsibilities and the legislation did not materialize.

Dr. Kieffer had been thinking a lot about associated
transportation problems; the proposed legislation was a partial
response. High speed rail was a great idea, but how were the people
to get to the stations? Jerry Kieffer discovered, as so many others
had, that existing transportation systems were sadly inadequate;

they typically are too expensive, provide poor service, and cannot cover the area adequately. In fact, the conclusion has been reported before and since by many studies, that continuing to build existing systems in *any amount* will not alleviate our transportation problem. Sad to say, this consensus, which is highly documented and readily available in the transportation literature, has yet to be heeded by the majority of transportation planners. Jerry Kieffer mulled over this problem at great length.

Just about that time (1968), Kieffer was named by Governor Tom McCall of Oregon to lead a major state reorganization study. He and his study body (Project 70's Task Force) were very successful in gaining both the governor's and the legislature's approval of wide-ranging changes in Oregon's state government. One of the changes was creation of a state Department of Transportation and a transportation bill including the creation of an Urban Transit Division. Kieffer's simple idea was that the new department would need a unit—the Urban Transit Division—to manage the allocation of Federal grant funds to Oregon's communities.

As soon as the bill was signed into law, an officer of a Portland/Vancouver community study group called Kieffer and asked him to come before the group and enlighten it on "the agenda of the new Urban Transit Division". He couldn't refuse, but simply to tell them that the agency would exist to dole out federal money wouldn't be much of a speech.

What to do? In January, 1969, not too long before he was to give his speech in Portland, Kieffer and his wife went to one of Oregon's fine ski resorts for a short vacation. There, in an illuminating moment, he became one of a handful of people around the world who have independently conceived of what today is called personalized rapid transit. His story of his experience at the resort is best described in a letter to the author, part of which is reproduced below, as follows:

> "I cannot exactly explain it, but on watching the ski tow
> vehicles moving past, my mind exploded in questions about

transit. Why do people have to travel in big transit cars attached to each other in long trains? Long trains require long, expensive station platforms. Why can't they travel in very small vehicles moving singly to the specific destination of their choice, bypassing all intermediate stops and go from origin to destination without stopping to pick up/drop off other passengers along the way? Why couldn't stations be located on short spur tracks off the main line, so vehicles on the main line not going to a particular station could bypass it on the way to their ultimate destination station? Why couldn't the vehicles be small and inexpensive, carrying 3 to 4 passengers traveling together by choice (no strangers)? If the vehicles were small, couldn't the great expense of big, heavy-duty, highly visible guideways be avoided? Why couldn't small guideways be up in the air, to avoid many of the complications of at-grade traffic movement? If the entire cost of such personalized transit could be brought way down, wouldn't that make possible the spreading around of transit service to meet the largely unserved transit needs of the medium/lower density areas that increasingly dominate the world's metropolitan settlements? If transit costs could be drastically reduced, couldn't many community systems avoid big deficits or even make money? Wouldn't it help attract to the transit field more investors if the scale of risk capital needed would be kept small?

Up to that mind explosion moment, I had never heard the words "personal rapid transit", and I had no idea whether anyone else in the whole world had asked these questions and developed a concept responsive to them. On getting home to Eugene, I quickly framed my speech on a now imaginative agenda for the new Oregon Urban Transit Division. At a televised speech to the community leadership group, I outlined my idea of the type of personalized transit system and service needed by a sprawling area such as Portland/Vancouver. The speech and the Q/A period were well received. When the speech was over, the leader of a television crew came up to me and reported that what I was proposing was actually being worked on somewhere. He recalled seeing a report on it that had come to his office. I went there with him where he found a report on a PRT system that was prepared by some people at the Stanford Research Institute. I was overjoyed! He gave me the report, which I read with amazement as I compared its system elements with what I had conjured up under the ski tow."

Jerry Kieffer had independently discovered nearly all of the basic tenets of personal rapid transit. Since that moment, his zeal for PRT has not diminished. But he was very busy in Oregon as chief spokesman for the governor's reorganization programs, and running his public policy and administration programs at the university. He had little time to think about PRT.

In the late summer of 1969, Dr. Kieffer accepted a new job that required him to move back to the Twin Cities: the directorship of a new national educational foundation that would be based in St. Paul. The foundation was funded by DeWitt Wallace, co-publisher of the Readers' Digest. The purpose of the foundation was to distill information from campus leaders who had successfully dealt with campus unrest, and disseminate these findings to other academic leaders. The job was too intriguing to pass up. He made the move to the campus of Macalester College at St. Paul, Minnesota.

It was thus almost inevitable that the paths of two of the greatest exponents of PRT, Dr. Jarold Kieffer, a public policy and management specialist, and Dr. J. Edward Anderson, an inventor and a mechanical engineering professor at the University of Minnesota, would cross.

Without knowing each other, both became members of the Transportation Committee of the Twin Cities area Citizens League, a community issues study group with influential membership drawn from the business community, the area's campuses, and government agencies. Kieffer described their meeting to the author as follows:

> "There [at the Citizen's League] one evening, I found my-
> self sparring lightly with a fellow down at the end of the
> table. As the evening progressed, I began to realize that he
> and I were actually closer together in our thinking than the
> two of us were to anyone else in the room during a lively
> discussion about transit ideas. At the end of the meeting I
> went over and invited this fellow to join me for a drink. He
> agreed, and that is how I met Ed Anderson."

At this private session, Anderson and Kieffer could hardly believe how close they were in their ideas about PRT and its characteristics. Yet, there was a key difference. Kieffer's concept required a line switch that would allow PRT vehicles to move freely from line to line, so as to permit a nonstop trip from origin to destination. Anderson, at that time, and as an engineer, hadn't yet conceived of a switch that would allow such easy line switching. Kieffer wrote to the author, as follows:

> "As a social scientist and public policy analyst, I knew how
> PRT ought to work in order to offer its greatest service ad-
> vantages. My cavalier attitude was: 'So, we must have a
> switch that allows the vehicles to move easily from line to
> line.' Ed, as an engineer, had to satisfy himself that such a
> permanently reliable and safe switch was indeed feasible.
> Until it was designed, he couldn't include it in his PRT
> concept. So, we agreed to differ on that point. However,
> soon Ed discovered on a trip to Germany that the Cabintaxi
> system had a switch that did allow line switching. On his
> return, he came to my office, threw his hat on the table, and
> proclaimed: 'Jerry, the switch exists; I saw it work!' From

that point on, we had no differences in how we perceived PRT. However, in his solid engineering way, he went on and developed an even better line switch, which, with support from the University, gained a U.S. patent and now is a key feature of the Taxi 2000 PRT concept."

During 1970, Drs. Anderson and Kieffer became fast friends. They were a team which accomplished the only progress made by PRT in those days. It was then that they received their indoctrination into just how intransigent public officials can be in regard to new developments. Their focus was criticism of the planning being done by the Twin Cities Area Metropolitan Transit Commission (MTC).

The Twin Cities, as well as the new suburbs reaching out 10 or more miles in all directions, were poorly served by public transit. With auto congestion already serious, and projected to get much worse in the next 20 years, what was needed was planning that focused on how to spread public transit much more widely than in just a few corridors.

Yet, a consultant firm's report on long range transit planning needs recommended that the Metropolitan Transit Commission (MTC) stress very costly heavy rail development in a few corridors in the whole metropolitan area.

The expensive rail response proposed by the consultant firm was so blatant that Anderson and Kieffer felt that they had to make a strong statement about it. When the MTC held hearings on the consultants' report, Anderson and Kieffer appeared to testify against it. The resourceful duo had managed to obtain a copy of the consultant's report to the MTC, and effectively used it against them. They were amazed at what happened. Jerry Kieffer described to the author the outcome of the hearing as follows:

"For this widespread, essentially medium/lower density metropolitan area, the consultants proposed a very costly heavy

rail line capable of serving only a very limited area. We expected such a proposal and decided to oppose it at a public
hearing. I would discuss the inappropriateness of the proposal in service terms for an area like the Twin Cities. Ed
would focus on its technical deficiencies and high costs. He
found an incredible statement made by the consultants themselves in an attachment to their report. It noted that even 30
years later, the line would carry only tiny percentages of
daily trips. We went to the hearing and made our com-
ments. To our astonishment, it was like throwing a rock at a
battleship, and the ship sank! The report died from neglect.
The Commission couldn't agree on what to do next. The
executive director and several staff members quit. For a year
the Commission stayed divided on the guidelines it should
follow in recruiting a new director. The governor then
stacked the Commission in favor of heavy rail, but Ed and
others got legislative action that took away from the Commission its planning function. Over 20 years later, the Twin
Cities still lacks an effective transit strategy."

Although in disarray, the MTC managed to stall the efforts of
Anderson and Kieffer. In the weeks following the hearing, Anderson and Kieffer tried to get support in the MTC for a study of
more effective transit options for the metropolitan area, including
PRT. However, the MTC members in favor of rail were too strong
to permit that to happen.

Kieffer Knocked out of Action

At this time in his career, Jerry Kieffer nearly lost his life. He
was the victim in Washington, DC of an automobile accident of
the most grievous proportions. He suffered multiple fractures of

his left knee and femur, as well as skin wounds and other trauma. He was confined to a Bethesda hospital, flat on his back for 90 days, trussed up in a traction device. Then, when traction failed to help his left femur heal, he had to be put in a full body cast. At that point, his wife arranged for his air transport to a hospital in the St. Paul area, near to where he lived. He remained in body casts for another 90 days. When his femur healed and the body cast was removed in May, 1971, he had no muscle power left at all in his legs. With help from the doctor and trainer of the Vikings football team, he had to be taught how to walk again. It took from May to July, through painful exercise and exhausting practice, just to be able to walk a half a block with crutches.

Throughout Kieffer's hospitalization in Maryland, weekly phone exchanges with Ed Anderson kept him in touch with Ed's thinking and actions, especially relative to the MTC. After Kieffer, enclosed in his cast, returned to St. Paul in January, 1971, they often met at his hospital bedside, continuing their collaboration.

The Only Paper in "English"

In July of 1971, still recovering, Kieffer went to Seattle to an engineers' conference. Earlier that summer, Ed Anderson and he had been invited to present papers on PRT for this joint conference of the American Society of Civil Engineers and the American Society of Mechanical Engineers. Each man had prepared a paper on the subject and sent it off for advanced distribution at the sign-up desks at the conference hotel. Kieffer's paper, "The Success of the Auto Should be Lesson to Us," analyzed the features of auto use that had made autos so successful in meeting the needs of increasingly widespread metropolitan area inhabitants. Kieffer called for new modes of transit that incorporated as many of these features as possible.

When Kieffer came to the conference hotel, the desk clerk

surprised him by saying: "You are very popular!" He then handed Kieffer a clutch of "Please Return my Phone Call" slips, all from media representatives. When Kieffer called one of them, he was told that the reporters as a group wanted to interview him about his conference paper. A little while later, after he met with them and answered their questions about PRT and other transit-related issues, he asked them why they had decided on a group interview with him. Their puzzling answer: "Your paper is the only one in English!" They explained that most of the other papers were written in heavy engineering language, with page after page of equations and other complicated terms of reference. They said that first they were attracted to the title of the paper, and then they found its pages full of simple, understandable English. Indeed, Kieffer, who had no background in engineering, had written the only paper which was understandable to a layman. In 1972, Kieffer's paper also became the lead chapter in "Personal Rapid Transit," published by the University of Minnesota's Institute of Technology. The book was one of the first transportation technology books that focused entirely on PRT. His paper also became the basis of one of a series of articles that appeared in the "Futurist" in early 1973.

A New Career in Washington

Dr. Kieffer went on to serve his country illustriously in many other important posts. While he was struggling with his efforts to walk again, Kieffer had to face a financial and career problem. Several months before Kieffer's near fatal accident in Maryland, DeWitt Wallace, the major benefactor of Macalester College, for reasons still unknown, decided to take the college out of his will and withdraw all current financial support for the college. The college trustees were forced to take the money from the foundation Kieffer directed and all other funds not spent and use them to sustain the college during the severe retrenching that had to take place. Kieffer had accepted a request from the trustees that he become their executive officer, to help them go though the reorganization. However, after the accident, flat on his back in traction in a Maryland hospital, he obviously was unable to help the trustees.

Therefore, by July, 1971, Kieffer needed to get a new paying job. At that point, at the suggestion of White House staff, he was invited to Washington for a series of job interviews. Although still frail and weak, Kieffer decided to leave his crutches home and use two canes instead. In mid-July, he saw Dr. John Hannah, then Administrator of the Agency for International Development (AID), and was offered a job. He also had a tentative offer as executive director of the Bicentennial Commission. He would have been responsible for guiding the planning and management of the program leading up to the 1976 celebration of the bicentennial of the American Revolution. However this exciting possibility turned out to be misrepresented, and he accepted instead the job at AID. He reported for duty in early September, 1971. Shortly, he was named by the president to become one of the assistant administrators of AID. He stayed on in that role until early 1975.

During his stint with AID, he had an interesting meeting in October 1972 with the President of Costa Rica, Jose Maria Figueres. In talking earlier in the day with the First Lady about auto/bus congestion, Kieffer mentioned the PRT idea. She was so taken with the concept that, on the spot, she arranged for him to sit next to the President's box at the opera that evening. During intermission, the president asked him to explain PRT to him and to his Minister of Transportation. They were quite interested. However, it was another case of interest being generated before a viable PRT system was available. But the seed has been sown.

After the hitch with AID, he was chosen to be staff director of a body established by Congress to study the operations of the National Institute of Health and the National Institute of Mental Health.

In the spring of 1976, he became Deputy Commissioner of Social Security in the Ford Administration. He served with distinction in that role until 1977, when Jimmy Carter became president and selected his own appointees.

Thereafter he served in a number of posts, ultimately being appointed in 1980 to be staff director of the 1981 White House Conference on Aging. He served in that role in the last year of the Carter Administration and through the first year of the Reagan Administration. In early 1982, he left government service and became a policy and management consultant in a number of fields, most notably in transportation.

During almost his entire career, Kieffer remained closely involved with the field of public transit. He took time to encourage greater public interest in searching for lower cost modes of transit that could be deployed much more widely.

Firmly Committed

Jerry Kieffer continues to actively pursue his championship of PRT. One of his themes is the aging population. He points out that not only in the U.S. but worldwide, populations are rapidly aging. The number of those over age 75 is growing the fastest. Yet, most of these older old people are still physically alert and desirous of remaining active and involved in community life. However, increasing numbers of them don't drive anymore; they have to depend upon others for travel. Increasingly they are marooned and isolated. Kieffer argues that, from both cost and humane concerns, provision of easily accessible, low cost transportation in our spread-out communities is one of the best strategies we could adopt.

In the past decade, Jerry Kieffer has written many thinkpieces and newspaper articles. He has spoken extensively at conferences to encourage policy makers and planners to recognize the critical need for new, very low cost modes of transit, such as Taxi 2000. He remains a vital force within ATRA, serving as Chairman of the Board of ATRA until he stepped down in January, 2000. He continues on ATRA's board as he has for the past 24 years. Recently, he was asked to lead another ATRA inquiry into the practical status of PRT development and costing.

Jerry Kieffer continues to be the guiding light of PRT development. He remains convinced that the world's traffic-congested metropolitan areas will not be able to cope with growing congestion without adopting very low cost, off-the-road transit modes that can permit many people to have a practical alternative to road vehicles. He regularly produces papers on the subject, such as his May 31, 1997 paper entitled "The Futility of Washington Area Transportation Strategies", in which he encourages the acceptance of new ideas. He never misses an opportunity to explain how PRT principles could be the answer, provided its builders keep costs as low as possible by using small vehicles, thin, aerial guideways, and small, widely-dispersed stations. It is no overstatement to say that the progress of PRT in its present state of evolution is due in no small measure to the unflagging zeal and dedication of Dr. Jarold A. Kieffer.

Chapter 21

Advanced Transit Association

The Vision

In Denver, in 1975, at the Third International Conference, Jerry Kieffer joined with Ed Anderson and others in calling for establishment of a special professional association. Its purpose was to encourage engineers, planners, and social scientists to foster public education on the need for higher service, lower cost, automated transit systems that could be affordable for widespread use in metropolitan areas.

The outgrowth of that effort was the establishment of the Advanced Transit Association (ATRA), with Ed Anderson as its first president and Jerry Kieffer as a member of the Board of Directors, a position he has held ever since. At that time, Kieffer had received his appointment to his Social Security post. In a letter to the author, he recalls an exchange at the first meeting:

> "In the early years, I probably seemed to be a fish out of water in that group. At the first ATRA board meeting, in 1976, I found myself sitting next to Michael Powell, executive vice president of a big international transportation consulting firm. He asked: "What the hell is the No. 2 guy in Social Security doing here?" After I explained my long-time interests in better urban transit, and my various govern-

YDE

ment positions relating to it, he apologized for his question,
and we became close collaborators in many ATRA matters."

In the years following, ATRA has become a major force in
fostering the development of new transportation systems. In its
role of nurturing development, it is open to *all* ideas which are
brought forward, even those which are quite fantastic and unworkable. As a neutral organization, it must treat all concepts with
respect. But ATRA has served a very useful purpose in developing
new transportation systems.

The ATRA Report on PRT

In January, 1988, when Dr. Kieffer was Secretary/Treasurer of
ATRA, he proposed an ATRA-sponsored conference for the specific purpose of evaluating the status of thinking and action about
PRT. He relates that the Association itself appeared to be adrift
and internally torn over the directions to be pursued. In particular, he noted a growing bitterness among some ATRA's members
as to the merits and prospects of PRT. He urged that ATRA do an
in-depth study to seek out the latest facts about PRT's developmental status and prospects, and make a fresh assessment of its
effectiveness. The board agreed that, despite ATRA's neutral stance,
the pro's and con's of PRT ought to be studied, so the chairman,
Thomas H. Floyd, Jr., was asked to convene the investigation. Floyd
agreed, but he wanted no charge by anyone that the committee
was biased in any manner. He put together a committee which
was a careful balance of thirteen engineers and consultants, some
in favor, some opposed, and some undecided.

PRT was carefully defined by listing the well-known characteristics of a good PRT system. The group was surprised to find
itself in agreement on these criteria, a list which remains ATRA's
test of good PRT design to this date.

Only two firms had concepts that fit the committee's PRT criteria: Cabintaxi, and Ed Anderson's Taxi 2000 Corporation. The submission by Cabintaxi consisted of a German language document and a 1979 videotape. In fact, the Cabintaxi representative stated that the Cabintaxi data was a lot of interesting but out-of-date history in file boxes. Since no further work had been done on Cabintaxi, the committee chose to focus on the Taxi 2000 system, which was presented to the committee by Ed Anderson.

After his presentation and a lengthy question and answer period, technical committee members were deeply impressed. The development of microprocessors, miniaturization, and computer-managed controls systems had markedly increased the feasibility of automated management of large fleets of small vehicles. When the committee finished its inquiry, no important dissent remained on this issue. However, as no Taxi 2000 system actually had been built and demonstrated in practical use, some members were somewhat skeptical about validating its claimed capacity, reliability, and, particularly, its very low costs. Chairman Tom Floyd's leadership proved to be the key to avoiding serious disagreements and dissents on this score.

Floyd came up with the idea of asking two experienced transportation system executives to provide their opinions as to Taxi 2000's overall technical feasibility and costs. To this end, Kieffer gained the help of Michael W. Loeffl, Vice President for Projects for the international transportation consultant firm Davy McKee, and of Richard Radnor, who had retired the year before from the Raytheon Company as one of its top control system engineers.

Loeffl wrote to Kieffer that the Taxi 2000 system was "sound and within the state of the art". He noted that every aspect of Taxi 2000 had been subjected to technical analysis by Davy McKee departments and had been subjected to a full cost review by its cost estimating department.

Radnor went into detail about Taxi 2000's control system, and in his letter to Kieffer wrote: "Completed costing studies for both the development and production show that a safe, reliable system can be developed and produced at a reasonable cost. I see no area where the state-of-the-art in electronic control need be advanced to make Taxi 2000 an operating system."

Floyd and Kieffer collaborated on writing the technical committee report, with Floyd successfully negotiating especially sensitive passages and conclusions with members who had been most dubious about PRT. While all members knew they could dissent if they wished to do so, Floyd and Kieffer were pleased that no critical point had to be compromised in order to get agreement. Considering the controversial basis for starting the PRT assessment the year before, Floyd and Kieffer were amazed at the degree of agreement by the end of the inquiry. Not a single dissent was filed! Amazingly enough, the doubters and the undecided ones were completely won over. When the study was concluded and the results published, the conclusions and recommendations were unanimous. The conclusions were positive in all areas: general feasibility, technical feasibility, economic feasibility, and public acceptance. Furthermore, the system was said to have great service potential and would be low in cost. The report was presented to the ATRA Board in January 1989, which endorsed it for worldwide dissemination.

The ATRA report attracted much attention in transportation circles and caused a surge of membership in ATRA. It also generated publicity and media interest in the PRT concept. The report had considerable influence on the decision of the Chicago area Regional Transportation Authority to make its ill-fated joint investment with Raytheon, but, of course, that fiasco is history.

ATRA continues in its pivotal role in examining and promoting advanced forms of transportation. It is the only organization to do so, either within or outside of the Federal government. PRT, as one of the advanced forms of transportation, has benefited greatly from the efforts of ATRA, and continues to do so.

Chapter 22

The Man Behind the Vision

The Career

On May 15, 1927, in Chicago, a son was born to two evangelical missionaries to China, C. Oscar and Ruth M. Anderson. The second of five children, he was named John Edward, but was known as Edward or J. Edward from childhood. He says of his citizenship that, although he was conceived in China, he was born in the United States. But he was to spend the next eight years of his life under precarious conditions in China with the missionaries, including capture of his father by the Communists.

The story of that life and the harrowing experiences his parents and their children underwent, first at the hands of bandits and later under the communists, is documented in *Two Lives of Faith,* the autobiographies of Edward's parents.

In 1936, the missionaries returned to the home of Ruth's mother in St. Paul, Minnesota, on furlough. After recuperating, they evaluated their position. Conditions in China were deemed hazardous, but tickets had already been purchased for the return to China in the summer of 1937. The Japanese invasion of Shanghai stopped their plans. By December of 1939 conditions were considered such that, although too hazardous for Ruth and the children, Oscar returned at the request of the Mission Board for a couple of years. There he survived the Japanese invasion and many severe bouts with various illnesses, and was not able to return to the United States until the late summer of 1944, when he was reunited with his family.

The China years are a vivid recollection to J. Edward Anderson, and his missionary background no doubt has contributed to his inner spirituality. He was graduated from high school in Chicago, did a stint in the Navy, and attended North Park College in Chicago, the institution at which his parents had met. This establishment has always had a nostalgic place in his heart, and in 1994 he delivered a speech there as the 1994 Distinguished Alumnus Lecturer, which, in this author's opinion, was one of his finest expressions. In this speech he details how he, in effect, received a calling from a higher authority to devote his life to some worthy cause. This speech is reproduced in full as Appendix B.

To understand how Dr. J. Edward Anderson has risen from humble beginnings to become the world's foremost expert on a technology which will ultimately make an historic and revolutionary contribution to the world society, it is important to step back and see his whole career.

In his early years he seriously considered following his parents' footsteps into the ministry. Whether or not Providence had other plans for his life is not known, but he eventually decided that his love of things mechanical and scientific would lead him to useful service in this world.

He received his bachelor's degree in mechanical engineering from Iowa State in 1949, his master's degree in the same field from the University of Minnesota in 1955, and his doctorate from the Massachusetts Institute of Technology in 1962.

After receiving his undergraduate degree he went to work at Langley Field, Virginia as an Aeronautical Research Scientist under NACA. But it wasn't long (two years) before he joined the Aeronautical Division at Honeywell, Inc. in 1951. His talents as an engineer were soon recognized. During his twelve years at Honeywell he rapidly progressed from Work Director to Senior Research Engineer, to Principal Research Engineer, to Research Staff Engineer, to Manager of Space Systems. At the height of his career at Honeywell, he had teams of engineers working under his direction to solve some of the important space problems of the time. However, much of this work related significantly to the industrial-military complex.

It was during his employment at Honeywell that he was able to avail himself of the opportunity to gain his doctorate. He took a two and a half year sabbatical from Honeywell and went to the Massachusetts Institute of Technology, working on his degree from 1959 to 1962 under a Convair Fellowship. In his work for his Ph.D., he studied special and general relativity theory, and independently solved the problem of clock paradox in general relativity. His mathematical acumen may be seen in many of his more than ninety papers, most of which relate to PRT. In these papers, he often submits the subject relentlessly to rigorous mathematical analysis and graphic presentation, which PRT passes extremely well.

J. Edward Anderson could have remained in a lifetime career at Honeywell, secure in the knowledge that his talents as an engineer and a scientist, as well as his faculty for coordinating and directing subordinates, were well appreciated. But he had reached a turning point in his life. He wanted a change. He wanted to make a difference of another kind in the world. He wanted to leave the world of designing the instruments of war, which activities had begun to weigh heavily on his conscience.

In 1963, he resigned from Honeywell. He gave up a secure position, the approbation of his peers, and rapidly increasing recognition for an insecure position, for no peer acknowledgment, and for a cause which he knew was there but which he had not yet recognized or defined. It was a leap of faith most of us would not be capable of making.

Anderson had always wanted to teach, and his higher education and experience easily qualified him. He applied for and was accepted as Associate Professor, Department of Mechanical Engineering, University of Minnesota. He was in essence almost starting all over again. He says of this period of his life that he was "low man on the totem pole."

In 1967 and 1968 he was a National Academy of Sciences Exchange Professor in the Soviet Union, where he had spare time to think and write. He became aware of the interdisciplinary nature of many of the problems facing mankind today, and that perception has served him ever since.

The Lead into PRT

In 1968, he returned to Minnesota unsure of what the future would hold. His teaching work was fulfilling to some degree, but he realized it would never fulfill the urge he felt strongly to be involved with some important need of society. He even thought about resigning his associate professorship, although to what end he had no idea. While still in the Soviet Union, he had voiced his concern to his department head, Dr. Richard Jordan, and upon returning had written to him about his dilemma. The author is in possession of a copy of this handwritten letter, in which the distress he was experiencing comes through clearly.

"I don't think you ought to resign," Jordan counseled. "There are many opportunities for service within this institution. For example, I think you ought to consider this." He handed Anderson a paper. It was a request by the Urban Mass Transportation Administration for submissions of interdisciplinary proposals regarding the problems of urban mass transportation. "We could provide whatever latitude you would need to pursue this objective."

Ed's interest was immediately piqued. Here was a chance to explore a field which was in need of serious study and which embraced the interdisciplinary philosophy which he had recently come to appreciate. In retrospect, Ed has recognized that his department head's counseling and the UMTA request for studies led him into Personal Rapid Transit. Without these simultaneous stimulants, he would probably never have entered the field. Within two years, he was teaching a new course entitled *New Concepts in Urban Transportation*.

Since that first exposure, Dr. Anderson has served with great distinction as chair of many panels, committees, task forces and other organizations both in the field of advanced transportation and in other areas, and has been the recipient of many honors. His curriculum Vitae list of activities, honors, honorary societies, honorary listings, memberships, sponsored overseas travel, books authored or edited, statements before congressional committees, and publications runs many pages. He has authored over ninety papers, mostly in the field of PRT.

In 1969 Ed Anderson met Dr. Jarold Kieffer. Arriving in St. Paul, Minnesota to take up a position as director of a project underwritten by DeWitt Wallace of Reader's Digest, Kieffer was anxious to establish roots and to become involved with local issues. Unknown to each other, Kieffer and Anderson joined the transportation committee of the Citizen's League.

They discovered a compatibility which went far beyond that which they held with the other members. The bond of PRT interest soon cemented the relationship into one of enduring quality which extends to this day. They worked tirelessly together to try to gain acceptance for personal rapid transit.

In December of 1970 they attracted the attention of Bob Boyle, a popular figure at radio station KUOM. Boyle organized a meeting for legislators at which John Borchert, Geography Professor at the University of Minnesota and Director of the university's Center for Urban and Regional Affairs, presented concepts of urban growth, and Ed Anderson presented concepts of PRT. Senator Mel Hanson was very impressed by that meeting, and drafted a bill empowering the legislature to commit $50,000 to the Center to develop a proposal to demonstrate PRT. To the great surprise of the two collaborators, Anderson and Kieffer, the bill passed. But the power of the Twin Cities Area Metropolitan Transit Commission (MTC) was not to be underestimated. Despite the best efforts of the pair and of the interested legislators, it proved impossible to work with the hidebound MTC, which in its impeccable wisdom, was married to the idea that heavy rail was the answer to all of Minnesota's transportation problems. The concept of the bill was to move PRT along to the point where it could receive funding from the federal Government. Without the cooperation of the MTC, this was not possible. The grant, however, did enable the University to study PRT further, which greatly benefited Ed Anderson's continuing efforts.

Anderson's Unique Resolve

The grant through the University of Minnesota did provide Dr. Anderson with the funds necessary to continue his work. As a result of this funding, he was able to visit every PRT initiative, worldwide, from embryonic concepts to full-scale test facilities. It is the author's opinion that this exposure was a critical factor in the maturation of Anderson's approach to PRT. He learned a crucial lesson from these excursions. What he found from these visits, as well as from studying the literature of all that had gone before, was that they all shared a common flaw: the inventors, imbued with a sense of the importance of their ideas, had rushed on to develop the hardware which would embody their system without doing a systematic, critical review of *all* of the elements which make up a truly viable PRT system. Thus they all included an Achilles heel which would ultimately bring them down. For example, many of the inventors forgot or ignored the fact that snow accumulation could be a very serious problem, so they designed guideways which were ideal snow catchers. A number of these were actually built and tested, but did not prove marketable. Other inventors designed cars which were just a little too big (four or more occupants) to take advantage of the small size and low weight considerations which are an integral part of ideal PRT design. These facts are known now, but they were not clearly understood at the time.

As a result of these visits and accumulated studies, Anderson resolved, against what must have surely been a strong temptation, *not* to design a system of his own. He resolved to continue studying and accumulating data until he was positive that every possible avenue of error and been thoroughly explored and solutions found.

This was one of the pinnacles of Dr. Anderson's ascendancy, one of the reasons why he is today recognized worldwide as the leading authority on PRT. Without this resolve, he might have gone on to design a system possessing some hidden problem, and become just another paving stone on the road to PRT fulfillment.

One of the paths Anderson chose in following this self-imposed mandate was to prepare himself for and finally to publish in 1978 a textbook, *Transit Systems Theory*, which sought to address advanced transportation solutions from the viewpoint of the problems to be met, rather than from the viewpoint of the introduction of a particular set of hardware. This was the only textbook of this nature ever to be published, before or since. It addressed the shortcomings of existing forms of transportation, and pointed the way to advanced forms which logically led to the development of PRT, but it did not actually specify the exact design of a PRT system. However, the mathematics utilized in the design of guideways and vehicles requires a good grounding in undergraduate math. It is well documented with numerous references to existing transportation literature. Anderson used it effectively in his classes at the University of Minnesota and also at Boston University. Other educators have also used this book, and it is still in demand today. While it was revolutionary in the type of viewpoint it presented to his students, it no doubt also helped Anderson, to a remarkable degree, to shape his own thinking.

Although he was completely immersed in PRT work by this time, Ed Anderson continued in his other fields of interest and expertise. As late as 1979 he was still involved in his assessment of the U. S. involvement in the arms race. He begun debating the usefulness of the MX missile at that time, and received national recognition as an expert in this field. In a regular broadcast of the

National Press club, transmitted by over 1200 stations, he spoke against the MX missile deployment.

Ed Anderson and Jerry Kieffer have continued their close association and cooperation to this day. They went on to work together to produce the international conferences on advanced transportation in general and PRT in particular which have been so instrumental in crystallizing the accumulated ideas into workable solutions. It is no doubt true that each would say of the other that he has been indispensable in the development of PRT.

As the recognized world leader in PRT, Ed Anderson has been paid the ultimate compliment by many authorities. Catherine Burke, in her expansive work, *Innovation and Public Policy*, states that Anderson has gained the reputation of being the leading supporter of PRT in the nation—the product champion. Steven Gluck, manager of the Raytheon PRT effort, speaking about Ed Anderson at the 1996 International Conference on PRT, said, "The basic concept of self-directed vehicles operating on a passive guideway, affording direct travel on demand, has been preserved because of the clarity and persistency of the world's leading advocate of the technology."

It is a role he fills with distinction, with eminent qualifications, and with great humility.

Chapter 23

Taxi 2000 and its Predecessor

To Design at Last

Although the guiding principle around which Dr. J. Edward Anderson formulated his philosophy with respect to PRT was one of forbearance and patience in designing his own system, time and accumulated knowledge eventually had their effect. The time came when he felt that virtually all of the problems inherent in good PRT design were known to him, and, furthermore, that he was in command of solutions which, if not perfect, were adequate to produce a feasible PRT system which would overcome the deficiencies of previous designs and result in a workable system.

He would be among the first to say that today we have capabilities, particularly in fault-tolerant dual-redundant computer technology, which far exceed that which was available in those early days. Yet he would maintain that a workable system could have been built at that time which would have had all the characteristics of good PRT design.

In June of 1982, the University of Minnesota awarded Anderson a $100,000 patent development grant. Working with Tony Patami, the University's Research Administrator, and Dr. Roger Staehle, Dean of the Institute of Technology, a concept was formed to develop the patents and commercialize the system.

Under this umbrella of the University of Minnesota facilities, Anderson developed designs which were unique in PRT state of

YDE

the art. He filed for five patents, each of which was granted, which represented giant steps forward in PRT technology. Of these, the most important was undoubtedly his onboard switch. While the benefits of the onboard switch had been recognized by others, notably William Alden in the design of his StaRRcar, and by the German system Cabintaxi, it remained for Ed Anderson to refine this switch so that it was eminently simple, reliable, and safe. His design has never been improved upon.

Anderson's onboard switch is a marvel of simplicity and effectiveness. In essence it consists of a single bar which is pivoted at its center and has a wheel at each end. The bar is mounted transversely on the vehicle carriage. There are two vertical running surfaces for switching purposes on opposite sides of the guideway. The switch is so arranged that, if one wheel engages the outside of its running surface, the second wheel is free. When the switch is thrown (by electromagnetic means), the second wheel engages the other surface, and the first one swings free. The switch snaps from one position to the other; there is no neutral position. Thus the car is constrained to hug one side or the other of the guideway. At a diverge point, it will follow the guidance of the engaged wheel.

Automated Transportation Systems, Inc.

If only the attempts at corporate structuring had been as successful for Ed Anderson as were his patents and designs! Unfortunately, the success of the former has proven over some eighteen years to be elusive, and time and again has escaped the principals, all of whom had the best interests at heart and devoted much time and energy to the cause.

By 1983 the first plans to organize were jelling, and, with the backing of the University, a company, Automated Transportation Systems (ATS), was incorporated. Joseph Shuster, a successful Minneapolis businessman, was one of the initial potential investors.

John McNulty, a St. Paul attorney, was brought on board. There was a perception, though by no means universal, that Ed Anderson, while a fine inventor, scientist, and professor, was perhaps not the right person to head up the new company.

Richard Gehring, who had served as President of Univac and had just retired as Executive Vice President of Sperry Corporation, was a friend of John McNulty. He was offered the job of President and CEO which he accepted with enthusiasm. It was felt that now all the necessary elements were in place: a revolutionary new product, patent protection, the experience and designs of the world leader in PRT technology, and an experienced CEO. Under Gehring's leadership, a private placement stock offering was launched.

It turned out, however, that the marketplace determined that all ATS really had was an idea, and example after example has proved that the public is not attracted to something which is nothing more than an idea. The stock offering was not successful; it did not begin to raise the funds necessary for the anticipated work of the company.

Richard Gerhing stayed on for some time, but eventually it became apparent that his experience in large corporations was not commensurate with the needs of a start-up company like Advanced Transportation Systems, Inc., so his resignation was accepted.

The resignation of Gehring as President and CEO and John McNulty as Board Chairman was precipitated in 1984 as a result of Automated Transportation Systems, Inc.'s becoming involved with the Davy McKee Corporation, whose president, Bob Perry, was an acquaintance of Joe Shuster, one of the original investors in ATS. Perry liked Shuster and was extremely interested in Ed's invention. An agreement was reached whereby Anderson would work full time at the Davy McKee offices, provided, however, that the company be reorganized. Perry was not impressed with the leadership of ATS, Inc. Thus it was that Roger Staehle was elected President, Chairman, and CEO.

This period from May 1984 to July 1985 was one of quite productive work for Ed Anderson in further developing and improving the design, while working with the company's cost-estimating department to develop costs for the entire system. As with other involvements, the hitch with Davy McKee Corporation served to further the refinement of Anderson's concept of PRT, but it did not lead to any actual testing or installation.

Taxi 2000, Inc.

Thereafter there followed a sequence which was so bizarre as to be almost unbelievable, and which nearly cost Anderson control of the company and of his invention. Roger Staehle, in good faith and with the company's interests at heart, began negotiations in the fall of 1985 with two young entrepreneurs, Judd Berlin, son of Lee Berlin, former president of 3M's European Operations, and Stuart Watson, grandson of IBM founder Thomas Watson, as major potential investors. At first, they were interested in investing with Roger Staehle remaining as CEO, but advisors convinced them that Staehle should be removed. Berlin and Watson had gone to high school together in Paris, and possibly had ideas of leading a new company which could become as great as IBM. By January 1986, a deal was proposed. Berlin felt that the name should be changed to be recognizable in almost any language, should indicate what the system does, and should contain a hint of the future. The name Taxi 2000 was decided upon. This was the only positive step accomplished.

The proposal was that Stuart Watson would become Chairman of the Board and Judd Berlin would become President and CEO. Anderson, Potami and Staehle would stay on the board. The deal was tentatively accepted in March of 1986, and, thereby, except for the goodness of Providence, control might have slipped forever from Anderson and his coworkers.

The group was almost miraculously saved from this fate because Watson and Berlin, in working with their investment firm, decided that Taxi 2000's debt of about $500,000 was too great and that a new corporation would have to be formed. Watson's lawyers advised him that he and Berlin could not both lead the old corporation and form a new one. They were advised that the proper step would be to resign from their roles and positions as officers, and take charge of the new corporation. This they did in June of 1986. The three remaining board members elected Anderson as President, Chairman, and CEO, and control was regained.

Watson and Berlin were probably not to blame for what happened next. They had allied themselves with three other potential investors: Robert W. Baird Company, Milwaukee; the Super Steel Company, Milwaukee; and Unico, Racine, Wisconsin. All three of these were impressed with the potential of PRT. Unico had even gone so far as to build, at its own expense, a 100 foot section of track and a vehicle. Evidently they began to conceive of themselves as the main force behind the PRT momentum, with the Taxi 2000 people playing only an introductory role. It may be that Watson and Berlin were unable to control this delusion. In any event the newly-formed company, which now had only negotiating power with Taxi 2000, made an offer in July of 1986 which was so biased as to be unbelievable. The stockholders of Taxi 2000, which included Davy McKee Corporation and the University of Minnesota, were to receive 8% of the stock of the new company; Watson, Berlin and associates were to receive 92%.

One cannot help but wonder if the officials of Taxi 2000 were in a state of shock. Quite understandably, Tony Potami, representing the interests of the University of Minnesota, the owner of the patents and know-how, spurned the offer. Ed Anderson, representing the other stockholders, refused. The offer was so far from reasonable that the Taxi 2000 group declined to make a counter offer. There were no other reasonable offers forthcoming, and the entire momentum collapsed. Thus ended one of the most far-fetched episodes in the history of the company.

Boston University

Ed Anderson had become a good friend of Dr. Arthur Metcalf, one of the wealthiest men in Massachusetts, as a result of their mutual interest in opposing the MX missile. Their relationship involved Ed and his wife, Cindy, making extended stays as house guests of Dr. Metcalf, and many summers of sailing with Metcalf on his 60-foot ketch off Martha's Vineyard. Ed remembers Metcalf as a short, salty, white-bearded man who loved sailing and was very good at it.

The couple had been in Boston at the invitation of Dr. Metcalf to attend the opening of the Arthur G. B. Metcalf Science Center at Boston University which was to be held a few weeks after the Berlin-Watson deal was begun. When Anderson accepted, he was asked to bring his slides on PRT and to be prepared to present them to John Silber, President of Boston University, as well as his financial advisor. Stuart Watson who was invited also came to the presentation. In a rather unfortunate sequence, Silber saw that a tentative deal had been struck with Berlin-Watson and recognized that there was no room for Boston University. Ironically, the deal with Berlin and Watson fell apart not long afterwards.

Upon returning to Minneapolis in the fall of 1986, Anderson contemplated his future and the future of the project. He was now President and CEO of Taxi 2000, which had no earnings and was not in a position to pay him a salary. He had no recourse but to continue teaching. He felt that perhaps he should try to move to the Civil Engineering Department which had a Transportation Division. He discussed this idea with the new Dean of the Institute of Technology, Jim Infante. But Infante had another concern on his mind. He of course was aware of Anderson's extensive work on PRT, and he asked whether he intended to continue that work. When Anderson answered in the affirmative, Infante said that continuation of that work would not be within his understanding of the educational mission of the University.

This unexpected course of events triggered a turning point in Anderson's career. He certainly could not abandon PRT now that he had seen it through to this point, yet he had to support himself and his wife. As a tenured full professor, continuing to teach was a practical necessity.

After some soul-searching, he put in a call to John Silber at Boston University. He told him there was a "window of opportunity": the Berlin-Watson deal was dead, and Anderson said he was willing to go to Boston University as a visiting professor during which time he would negotiate a deal in which BU would raise the funds needed to develop Taxi 2000. Within a week Anderson had an appointment as a full professor in the Department of Aerospace and Mechanical Engineering. He resigned from the University of Minnesota and in late August flew to Boston to establish residence.

The professorship turned out very nicely. Anderson was able to teach courses in advanced transportation technology and in other related subjects. But the involvement of Boston University with Taxi 2000 did not.

In October, negotiations with Boston University began and were handled for Dr. Silber by his financial vice president Charles Smith. Smith apparently thought Anderson was coming hat in hand for any kind of deal, so in December offered a deal that would give BU five years to raise the necessary funds. He told Anderson to hand over all of his drawings, analysis, models, and computer programs and "maybe he would be made a consultant." When this untenable deal was turned down, Smith would not consider any kind of a counter proposal, and in fact wanted no more discussion.

At Boston University, Dr. Anderson taught courses from his textbook *Transit Systems Theory*. He organized and taught a course entitled *Technology and Society*, which is still taught today. All the while, he kept on doggedly working on furthering the cause of PRT, but remained at his post as a professor in the Department of Aerospace and Mechanical Engineering for many years. In fact, it was not until well after the potentially productive meeting with Gayle Franzen of the Chicago RTA in 1989 that he began to consider a move back to Minneapolis.

It has been stated elsewhere herein that PRT is the one form of public transportation which does not need a government subsidy; it can earn its own way through private capitalization. Taxi 2000, and its predecessor, Automated Transportation Systems, did make some valiant attempts at working directly with private investment. Some of the promoters of these schemes were charlatans whose exploits left the principals of the companies sadder and wiser. In some instances, personal greed raised its ugly head and precluded meaningful negotiations. Needless to say, none of the efforts resulted in the utilization of the technology. But is is probably true that Taxi 2000 emerged from these encounters more able to deal with venture capital overtures, and better equipped to formulate the right deal when the proper time would come.

Ed Anderson has persevered over this 30-year period in his intractable determination to see the actual realization of PRT. Not only is he the recognized worldwide authority on PRT, but also he is probably the world's person most anxious to have it fulfilled. It is interesting that, for good and valid reasons, none of the original or earlier players in this drama are still with him. In some cases, they turned out to be not quite perfectly suited for the role; in other cases, they were required to earn a decent living, which PRT could not yet provide.

Present Directorship

The Board of Directors of Taxi 2000 presently consists of three individuals in addition to Anderson, all of whom have known him for many years and are devoted to PRT. Chairman A. Scheffer Lang has known him since 1969, and has been an admirer and a strong supporter of Ed and of PRT through the years. He brings to the

Board not only his infectious and eternal optimism but also a vast number of other attributes, including his lifetime experience with the railroad and transportation industry. J. Bertram Press is a lawyer who has served Ed in a personal legal capacity for many years. His conservative sense and his cautions from a legal viewpoint are a valuable resource in the deliberations. Lastly, this author has known Ed Anderson and followed his career for nearly twenty years, and, as the reader might judge, is thoroughly imbued with the fantastic potential of PRT. Although not from the transportation industry, the author's fifty years of business experience may have some contributory value.

The University of Minnesota also has its representation. It awarded Anderson the $100,000 patent development grant and is the owner of the patents. The University fostered the growth and development of the original Automated Transportation Systems, and has been supportive of the successor company, Taxi 2000, throughout its history. It is the second largest stockholder of Taxi 2000. An important member of the Taxi 2000 team is Anthony Strauss, director of the University's Patents and Technology Marketing, who ably represents the interests of the University. Ed Anderson and Tony are old friends, and Tony has great respect for Dr. Anderson and his technology.

Since its incorporation, the Taxi 2000 name has been retained, and today it is synonymous in the minds of many PRT planners with the optimum PRT design. Dr. Anderson is President and CEO of Taxi 2000, the company which is the repository of all of his accumulated knowledge and the specifics of his designs. Although the company has weathered some control problems which were worrisome, Ed Anderson has remained at the helm as President and CEO. There have been several other instances where new major investors hoped to wrest control, and reward the inventor and the stockholders with a pittance. Since the Watson-Berlin ordeal, they have been stoutly resisted.

Chapter 24

With the Help of a Pro

The Genuine Article

There were quite a number of events which occurred during the career of J. Edward Anderson which are illuminating and revealing in regard to human nature. The conclusion one is forced to draw is that, in the implementation of any new idea, the vagaries of human nature can hardly be overstated as to the degree with which they can affect the outcome. Many of these stories, both humorous and grim, are documented in depth by this author in the biography of Dr. J. Edward Anderson, now being compiled for future release.

One of these, however, is so fantastic that it is deemed appropriate to lift it verbatim from that biographical work for this publication. The story follows in its entirety.

It was in Atlantic City that Ed Anderson had one of his most frustrating and, in retrospect, diverting adventures, or misadventures. Atlantic City had just made the decision to legalize gambling. It was hoped that this decision would restore the old grandeur to the faded and demoralized resort city.

The sequence of events happened during the period from 1977 to 1980, when Ed was trying valiantly to represent the German Cabintaxi system in the United States, and to find a large U. S. contractor willing to work on PRT under a licensing agreement with MBB and DEMAG, the two large German companies which in partnership developed the Cabintaxi system.

In the spring of 1978, Ed got a call from a Mr. Peter Karabashian, from Atlantic City: "Dr. Anderson, I'm the Director of Planning for Atlantic City. We're doing some important things here to kind of revitalize things. I've heard something about the German system for public transportation that I understand you represent. We're having a number of transportation representatives come here on June 5th to present their systems. Could you come out here and give us the pitch?"

Any new prospect was good news to Ed. He spent the morning of the 5th walking the proposed route and taking pictures, and, when his allotted 45 minutes came up, he made a good presentation on Cabintaxi to Karabashian and the other members of the Atlantic City Planning Board, including Commissioner Edwin Roth, who indicated great interest. Following the presentation, Karabashian asked Ed privately to step outside for a talk. He told him that they were very interested in Cabintaxi and that they were very serious. He expressed an interest in visiting Germany and seeing the test installation first hand. Ed felt assured that he had won out over the other contestants. The same day he wrote a five-page letter to Dr. Klaus Becker, the actual inventor and his Cabintaxi contact in Germany, outlining his progress and the steps that were needed to be taken.

In mid-August Ed got a call from a Mr. Sidney Kline, who said he was Director of the MMB Purchasing Office in New York.

"Dr. Anderson, I understand you are our U. S. representative for Cabintaxi."

"That's correct."

"Good. It took some time and quite a little effort to track you down. I wasn't familiar with Cabintaxi—MMB is a very large outfit, you understand—but I called my boss at MMB headquarters in Munich. They searched around and found that you are the representative."

"Well, I'm glad they keep good records."

"Do you know a Mr. Jim Ryan, of New York?"

"No, I don't think so."

"He was sorry he missed your presentation in Atlantic City. But some of the literature you left has the MMB name on it, so he looked me up. He's the one you should be talking to. He represents the casinos in Atlantic City. He's well-heeled; had me out to his home on Long Island; I was certainly impressed. And he knows financing and venture capital. I told him I would have you call him."

"Well, I certainly will. Thank you very much for the advice."

Ed put in a call as soon as it was expeditious. Jim Ryan was all that Sidney Kline said, and more. "Is this really *the* Dr. Anderson, of Minnesota fame?"

"I guess you could say that."

"I can't tell you how delighted I am that you called. I'm personally very excited about the possibilities of PRT."

"Well, that's good. Sidney Kline tells me you represent the casinos in Atlantic City."

"I do, and more than that, I can tell you they are unanimous in their desire to see PRT established there. They realize how important it could be in providing good transportation. Together with their move to legalize gambling, it would revitalize the city, in my humble opinion. I would love to see it happen. And I'm sure it can be done."

"Financing is one of the problems we run up against, time and time again."

"My friend, put your concerns to rest. There are venture capitalists who are actually looking for a good, adventurous investment. I can vouch for it."

"So that's your field?"

"You might say so, among other enterprises. One of my great joys is to see projects in which I have had a hand in organizing come to fulfillment."

"Your contribution sounds like just what we need."

"I'm sure of it. But you obviously need more than just my say-so. I would like very much to meet with you and some appropriate representatives of MMB and DEMAG at Atlantic City, where we can meet some of the developers, casino heads and city officials."

Ed would have liked to have had that meeting at once, but he was already committed to visit various University Industrial Engineering Departments per request of his Department Head. Jim Ryan wanted to keep in touch, so Ed called him from Georgia Tech, Virginia Poly, and Purdue, getting more of his in-depth knowledge of financial transactions and plans to expand the casinos in Atlantic City with each call.

As Ed recalls, "It was exactly what we were looking for."

In preparation for the meeting, Ed again contacted the head of the Cabintaxi project at DEMAG in Germany, Dr. Klaus Becker, who was an intense typical German engineer with a dueling scar on his cheek. He arranged for a couple of people from DEMAG to attend the meeting, along with Ed and Sidney Kline from MMB.

They met on September 26, 1978, at the Resorts International, the first casino to be opened under the new legalized gambling laws. When Ed arrived, Ryan and the Cabintaxi people were already in earnest conversation. Ryan simply exuded contagious enthusiasm. He was as suave and erudite as anyone Ed had ever met.

As Ed recalls it: "He was a thoroughly charming man with great knowledge of finance as well as the psychology of gambling, which he shared with us in great detail. He was a well-dressed slightly overweight man, probably in his late 40s, a handsome man of Irish decent who could have easily been a high-level corporate executive. After dinner, he took us on a tour of the vast 1000-table casino. The next day, he picked us up in his Cadillac and took us to the offices of several developers and casino owners with whom we discussed the project."

It was beginning to take on the aura of a very auspicious development, so much so, that the head of the New York office of Mannesman, parent company of MMB, felt obliged to become involved. He was a genuine German prince by the name of Peter Wittgenstein. Ed recalls: "We had a most engaging three hours together over dinner one evening. He was in his forties, black hair, and very distinguished features, but no mustache or beard."

Ed would get calls from Ryan regularly, sometimes from Atlantic

City, sometimes from Las Vegas. Ed's wife Cindy would sometimes take the call. He charmed her, too.

"Would this be Ed Anderson's spouse?"

"Yes, that's me."

"Do you treasure conversation with Ed as much as I do, or doesn't he talk shop at home?"

"Oh, he does, but maybe I enjoy just as much conversations on slightly different subjects."

"I can tell, just listening to you, and knowing Ed's consummate taste in all matters, that looking at you would not be too hard on the eyes."

And so on.

The degree to which Ed Anderson was beginning to depend upon Jim Ryan, and repeating his concepts and financing advice, is revealed in a letter he wrote Klaus Becker on September 30, four days after the meeting in Atlantic City with Ryan and the Cabintaxi people. A portion of that letter follows:

"The process of selection and implementation of a system in Atlantic City is unusual and not characteristic of other cities except Las Vegas. There, an important factor in failure of the system was the fact that the Rohr Corporation did not have a strong level of support from the hotel and casino operators. If Mr. James Ryan can accomplish this, a major breakthrough can be obtained. A key is participation and ownership of the AGT system by the hotel and casino operators so that they can use it as a tax deduction. If the city were to float municipal bonds which were bought by interests outside of this key group, there is little chance for success. On the other hand, it is clear that the hotel and casino operators badly need an AGT system able to provide a realistic alternative to the automobile and Cabintaxi is the only system able to do that. Considering the nature of the city, private financing is key. Having a man like Ryan committed to putting together all of the factions could be extremely useful not only for this project but for others. He is a wealthy man and knows his way around in financial and development circles and this is just the catalyst we need. He wants to be instructed on technical details and once he fully grasps the significance of the Cabintaxi system and sees how he can profit from its deployment we may have just the combination we need."

Things were going so well. Ryan's financial backers were in falling in line. The casino owners were behind the development. The cabintaxi people were very pleased that a U. S. installation was in the making. Ryan's expected commission for putting the deal together was a small fraction of the total cost, and, even though he needed it up front, and in cash so that he could cover his taxes due on other profitable deals which did not generate cash, it was a reasonable fee. The only nagging concern which Ed had was that Commissioner Edwin Roth, who had been so enthusiastic at that first presentation meeting, now seemed aloof. But, altogether, it seemed to Ed to be too good to be true. And of course it was.

Finally, the house of cards began to tumble. In retrospect, it seems incredible that a man of Ryan's acumen could have made the fatal blunders that he did. His first mistake was to tell Commissioner Roth that he represented Cabintaxi. By itself, this might have been acceptable; in a way, he did represent Cabintaxi through Ed Anderson. But Ryan had also called the Cabintaxi office in Germany, telling them that he represented the casinos. The German Cabintaxi office called Commissioner Roth to check out Ryan, and the double representation was discovered. This was the reason, Ed learned later, that raised suspicions in Commissioner Roth's mind, and turned him cool toward the proposed venture. In fact, the Atlantic City officials had begun to suspect that all was not well, but they felt it was not their place to reveal this to Ed; they felt he should learn this on his own.

Ryan knew that MMB and DEMAG were interested in

obtaining a large U. S. corporation to take on the Cabintaxi system. He made the mistake of calling the Vought Corporation and offering them the U. S. partnership with Cabintaxi for $1 million. If they had accepted, he could have told Ed he did it on Ed's behalf. Instead of accepting, however, an executive of Vought, Mr. Austin Corbin, called Ed and told him of the scam.

The third mistake Ryan made was at his meeting with Prinz Wittgenstein. They had agreed to meet in Atlantic City, so that Wittgenstein could check out the situation. During the conversation, he mentioned that one of Mannesman's many businesses was the manufacture and sale of large steel pipes that carried oil, and that they did business in Saudi Arabia. Always ready to show off his extensive contacts, Ryan said that he knew some of the Saudi princes. He pulled out a card which he said was a pass to the palace in Riyadh. But Prinz Wittgenstein was not fooled. He had been to Saudi Arabia, and recognized the card as an ordinary Saudi Arabian driver's license. Although he did not call Ryan's bluff, needless to say, the prince became very suspicious.

How could an accomplished con man such as Ryan have made such monumental blunders? One can only assume his towering ego required him to assert every possible self-aggrandizement.

But even without these mistakes, he would have fallen. Ed's own write-up on this episode, slightly edited, is revealing:

"I got a call from a *Wall Street Journal* reporter, Jonathan Kwitny, who asked me a long string of questions about my encounter with Ryan. I asked him what it was all about and he said that Ryan was out on bail for swindling some 20 contractors out of some tens of thousands of dollars each on a land deal in Africa. Kwitny had described the incident at some length in a *Wall Street Journal* article. I immediately informed Sid Kline and DEMAG of this call and of course all contacts with Ryan terminated.

"As a sequel, I called Sid Kline sometime in December

of that year sort of as a wrap-up call. He told me that he found a book on New York mobsters by Jonathan Kwitny entitled *The Fountain Pen Conspiracy*, in which there was a picture of a group of con artists including a smiling Jim Ryan standing next to one of the most notorious mobsters in New York. He then said that a woman friend of his happened to come into his office to say hello and asked what he was up to. Kline related the story of his adventures with Jim Ryan, and she exclaimed "Jim Ryan!" She said that she and her husband had "sold" their home on Long Island to Jim Ryan in a transaction in which he would pay for it from a commission he would soon receive on the sale of a new transit system in Atlantic City. Ryan was so genuine sounding that they let him move in without paying one cent. They were now in the process of getting the deal rescinded.

"Jim Ryan could have done very well as a top corporate executive, but he had a quirk in him that made the carefully crafted swindle irresistible. There was no greater joy for him than in inventing and carrying out his schemes, in which he would go to one party and say he represented the other, obtain some information and then go to the other party and say he represented the first. In that way, as Kwitny describes, he made a commission of about $600,000 on a sale of some ocean-front property in Atlantic City to Ramada Inns."

Such was Ed Anderson's introduction to the world of slick operators. The correspondence reveals that Ryan was asking the Atlantic City people for a $5,000 per month fee, which Ed did not learn about until much later. Ryan's capers were no doubt largely responsible for a telegram from Klaus Becker sent to Ed from Germany, which left little room for doubt that Ed was held responsible for not properly investigating Ryan. The relationship was badly damaged. Ed made a heroic attempt to reply to the telegram point by point with a three-page letter, but the correspondence does not indicate that he was successful. There may have been other factors also, but after the suspicion and distrust created by Ryan, there was no possibility of rescuing the Atlantic City project, and, even though the Cabintaxi executives and particularly Ed Anderson continued their efforts, it went down in defeat.

Although the Atlantic City project went down the drain, Ed Anderson continued to work with with Cabintaxi until the program was canceled in December of 1980. Ed went to Germany in the spring of 1979 for a transportation conference, and had warm, friendly discussions with Klaus Becker and others. However, although there were several tantalizing leads which developed in the States, nothing positive was forthcoming.

At the time, this and other defeats in respect to Cabintaxi seemed like crushing blows, but, as detailed elsewhere, they eventually turned out to be blessings in disguise.

Chapter 25

The PRT Facilitator

The Facilitator Defined

Looking into the future, it is instructive to contemplate how PRT systems will be built. It is anticipated that a Personal Rapid Transit company will serve as a facilitator. It will enable municipalities and other interested entities to pursue the possibility of installing a PRT system for its citizens or patrons. The term "facilitator" will be used hereafter to denote such a company, but it should be understood that various companies may evolve in the future which may not fit the mold herein portrayed. Moreover, it should be realized that we are moving here into uncharted waters. No one can predict with certainty at this stage what the actual course of development may turn out to be. The following description is, therefore, substantially of a conjectural nature.

A PRT facilitator is not in the manufacturing business, nor does it strive towards that as a goal. Even if it did, it could not begin to satisfy the demand for literally thousands of PRT vehicles, hundreds of miles of guideways, and hundreds of stations which will be needed as the transportation renaissance begins to come into full flower. These will need to be obtained from a wide diversity of suppliers.

A facilitator for a PRT system may be compared to an architect in the building industry who is also retained to supervise construction. The analogy is not perfect, but there are several

YDE

parallels. A facilitator has designed the PRT system; the architect has designed the building. The facilitator supervises the installation; the architect supervises the construction. The facilitator designates the suppliers and subcontractors; the architect does the same. In this analogy, however, there is no parallel to the control system provided by the facilitator, a non-replicable proprietary item which is the responsibility of the facilitator as to its maintenance and service.

However, the facilitator may assume a more-encompassing relationship with the customer by becoming the general contractor for the project, to whom all of the suppliers and subcontractors are responsible. In this role, the facilitator may best serve the needs of the customer, who may not wish to assume this role. It is important to recognize that, particularly at the outset of the transportation renaissance, no general contractor will have the experience and background necessary to fulfill this role, since PRT systems have never been built. The customer may well be more comfortable with the facilitator's acting in this capacity than with any other arrangement.

A further logical development may be that a facilitator may find it mutually advantageous to ally itself with a major corporation, perhaps one of the big names in American industry, who would in theory have the ability to fulfill all the functions of facilitator, manufacturer, and general contractor. Knowing the propensity of large corporations to want to control all aspects of an acquisition, and their engineers to want to take over the design, PRT companies may well question whether or not such an alliance may be easily forged. The following description will keep to the definition of facilitator already established. The description which follows would need to be substantially altered if an affiliation with a major corporation were to be consummated.

The customers, whether a city, a theme park, or an airport, are probably the ones who will own and operate the systems. However, it is possible that separate corporations may be established for the purposes of owning, operating, and maintaining the systems. The guideways and stations will be built by local contractors who are familiar with local ordinances and requirements; the customer is the one who will deal with the relationship of the contractors to those ordinances. The role of the PRT facilitator will be to supply the plans and specifications for the guideways, and the plans and specifications for those parts of the stations which are critical to proper operation of the system, such as the station siding and vehicle berths, the ticketing systems, the handling of vehicles needing servicing, and the storage tracks for idle vehicles. The actual physical design of the stations will be up to architects chosen by the customer to execute stations appropriate to the locale. Some stations, particularly in downtown locations, will be inside existing buildings. It will be up to local designers to harmonize such requirements with existing architecture. The exterior appearance of the guideways and supporting columns may be varied by the customer as desired.

The vehicles will be purchased by the customer on a bid basis, manufactured by various producers who will base their bids on the *exact* plans and specifications provided by the facilitator. The customer will have the latitude to determine cosmetic values, such as the color or finish of the cars, the interior fabrics, and seat cushion materials.

The control system components will likewise be purchased on a bid basis from those suppliers who wish to bid, again on the *exact* set of plans and specifications provided by the facilitator. This will very likely include products, model numbers, and brand names of specific component suppliers.

It is critically important that the customer realize at the outset that the above requirements are not subject to negotiation or variation. In order for the system to run properly, every operating element must be as specified by the the facilitator's system specifications, and the facilitator must reserve the overriding prerogative to reject bids which contain unauthorized substitutions for any operating element. Anything less rigorous, even of the most insignificant element, might jeopardize the proper operation of the system.

To accomplish this task, the services of a Procurement

Administrator who will insure that all purchasing functions are accomplished smoothly and with full compliance, and at the best possible price, will be provided by the facilitator. His experience with previous installations will be invaluable in this regard.

The standby power system is subject to less rigorous controls. So long as the standby system can deliver the required specifications of power within the specified time function, considerable latitude will be allowed for the customers to purchase the type of standby power supply they consider most appropriate for their use. The facilitator, however, must retain the unqualified right to reject any proposed standby power source it may consider unsuitable.

One of the most important elements provided by the facilitator is the computer simulation, which is a wonder of mathematical accomplishment. Not all facilitators may have the capability of providing such a simulation. These are exact replicas of proposed systems engineered for particular cities, down to the last detail. Since the simulations reproduce every function, they can be used to study intensively the proposed installation. The computer simulations are, in fact, secure editions of the actual code that operates a system, and will be used to configure all of the computers of the system.

Franchise Agreement Benefits

The customers will exercise a franchise or other binding agreement with the facilitator corporation to initiate the process of creating a PRT system.

The following benefits will accrue to a city or other customer executing such a franchise or agreement:

> They will receive full use of the the facilitator name, logo, and aids such as a virtual reality video, and advertising rights.

As a critical item, designed expressly for their particular system, they will receive a computer simulation. The simulation is invaluable in demonstrating the proposed system, and in configuring the actual computers of the system.

They will be absolved from the need to hire "experts" to advise them. Since practically all experts have gained their experience from existing transportation systems, they are of little help and could very likely be detrimental. This has been demonstrated time and again by various municipalities which have tried independently to investigate PRT.

They will receive conducted tours of one or more existing facilitator installations in other cities, with full explanation of all functions.

They will be disabused of the notion that it is feasible to design their system from scratch. They will have access to all of the engineering data of the facilitator with regard to all aspects. If problems develop, they will have the backlog of experience with systems of other cities which have the the facilitator program to fall back on.

They will receive the complete facilitator plans, diagrams, and specifications, enabling them to seek bids for the components. These documents will be copyrighted, and may be patented with design patents on the drawings and diagrams.

They will received the services of a qualified PRT Systems Engineer, who will work with them to establish the system's carrying capacity, and will lay out for them the system serving the area they desire. If they so choose, they can start with a small loop or two, expanding the system as they see fit.

They will receive the services of a qualified Procurement Administrator, who, working with the Systems Engineer, will develop the specifications for the number of vehicles, the station configurations, the control components and other elements from the computer simulation, which

were established from the carrying capacity and system layout. The Procurement Administrator will be entirely familiar with the product and the vendors, and will serve as the
customer's agent in obtaining the best prices and delivery,
and insuring that the quality is up to the the facilitator's
standards.

They will receive operating and maintenance manuals
and advice, as well as complete cooperation with the facilitator engineers until the system is up and running satisfacto-
rily.

They will have the written assurance that the facilitator's
engineers stand ready to serve them in the event of any
failure or disruption of the system, and ready to cooperate
fully in any expansion of the system which might be needed.

They will be within the mainstream of PRT design.
They will be a part of the growing body of client cities using
the facilitator's system. They will participate in the newsletters, share in the exchange of information relative to all the
aspects of operating and managing a PRT system of the
facilitator's design.

Subsidization

In the course of reviewing and contemplating the development of the phenomenon of Personal Rapid Transit, it seems apparent to this author that there is one salient factor which sets it
apart; one which has not been given nearly the recognition it deserves. That is that, of all the forms of public transportation yet
devised or implemented, *PRT is the only one which does not have to
be subsidized, in fact, which can make a profit!*

At first glance, this may seem like a nice feature but not really
of earthshaking importance. But it is. The reason is that because of
this attribute, PRT can be developed and financed by the free
enterprise system just as any other invention in any other field.

The greatest mistake which has been repeatedly made throughout the developmental history of PRT has been the notion that it has been necessary to obtain government approval and funding for PRT to succeed. This mistake has been the cause of innumerable setbacks and delays due to all of the shortcomings of government agencies. They have repeatedly been unable meet the "paradigm challenge" in accepting a revolutionary innovation, as defined and illustrated so thoroughly by Catherine Burke. Had the inventors of PRT systems realized that the profitability nature of the concept would allow them to develop PRT by means of venture capital, the story line of this book might have been far different.

In fairness, it must be noted that many inventors did not have the basics well enough in hand to be able to show that their products could yield a profit at the farebox, and, indeed, many of them could not have done so. This feature only emerged when the systems were so completely developed that costs were fully and accurately known, and factors like ridership, customer acceptance, competing fares and so on could be evaluated.

Ready for PRT?

Is your city, airport, or theme park ready for PRT? It is time to start the study process. Experience has shown that many meetings are the norm before a consensus can be reached and a PRT program initiated. A facilitator stands ready to meet with the proper authorities, at reasonable consultation fees, to begin this process.

One thing is certain. The time is ripe. Everything is in place. **The accumulated knowledge and techniques are available.** Once the first installation is made and the phenomenon becomes proven and widely known, people by the thousands will come from all over the world to see and ride on this new marvel. The worldwide production facilities will begin gearing up to provide the burgeoning needs of the transportation renaissance, and the world will never again be quite the same.

Appendix A

Why, After Decades, Hasn't Personal Rapid Transit Been Widely Accepted?

by J. Edward Anderson, Ph.D., P. E.
March 31, 1997

Introduction

I am frequently asked why, if PRT is such a good idea and has been considered for decades, it has not been widely accepted. This piece is intended to provide an answer.

In August 1974 as a result of heavy lobbying, the UMTA High-Capacity PRT Program was turned into a "harmless" and poorly funded technology-development program. Since then transportation consultants have advised city planners to look only at "proven" systems. Because of today's congestion, the cry repeatedly is that "we must do something" and the consultants advise again and again that that "something" is light rail (LRT), i. e., a modern version of the streetcar that was first introduced in the 1880's when the competition was a horse-cart on a mud road.

LRT is promoted as being efficient. If energy efficiency is implied, LRT is not a good choice. A study of available data shows that, because the daily average LRT load factors are rarely if ever more than 10 to 20%, LRT efficiency is roughly equivalent to an automobile system getting no more than about 10 mpg and is significantly worse than the energy efficiency of the average bus system. If land efficiency is implied, LRT would be efficient if all the lines could be placed on abandoned and available rail rights-of-way. If a new exclusive right-of-way is to be used, however, the costs go up to the range of $100 million per mile. If, as advocates urge, costs are reduced by placing the system on city streets, they must be placed on busy streets if they are to serve many people. Yet, LRT systems require typically a 38-ft right-of-way, thus reducing room for auto traffic by about two lanes in each direction. If the LRT system would attract as much travel as there had been with the existing auto lanes, it may be a good solution, but typically it attracts much less travel and thus it increases congestion. Moreover, many accidents are reported on surface-level LRT lines, which must be included in an overall calculation of efficiency.

LRT is promoted as the way to reduce congestion and air pollution. Yet ridership studies in auto-oriented U. S. cities show reductions in auto-miles of travel by LRT in the range of half of one percent. In an application I became acquainted with recently, the traffic flow in the recommended LRT corridor was reported to be 120,000 auto trips per day, in which case there would be about 12,000 trips per peak hour. One half of one percent of that is 60 auto trips per hour, or one per minute, yet the planner proudly asserted that the proposed LRT system could handle 40,000 persons per hour, which would be enormous and expensive overkill.

Why thus propose LRT? The planner argued that he was not permitted to take into account extra travel due to development he believes, with no supporting data, will occur in his corridor. Yet to produce such development would require zoning regulations that are not in place and are not likely to be in place because they would define where people could live. The hope some planners have of rearranging communities so that conventional rail transit will be economical is unrealistic. Yet LRT is strongly promoted, and when planners are asked about alternatives, such as PRT, the answer is usually a) don't look at anything not proven, and b) PRT does not have the capacity needed for the application.

And, as the reader knows, there is no work at the U. S. federal level to prove any new transit systems, notwithstanding rising transit deficits and huge amounts being spent on automated highway systems and their instrumentation. To make matters worse, other countries generally look to the U. S. for leadership and tend to follow what is done here.

> *"We are living at a time when one age is dying and the new age is not yet born." Rollo May*

Comments

UMTA was formed in 1964, not only to revive dying municipal bus companies, but to fund the deployment of BART-type rapid rail systems in cities all over the United States. Quite evidently lobbyists did not perceive that the new organization would get involved with new systems, but they could not stop placement of a paragraph in the UMTA Act that directed that new systems be studied. I recall a vice president of one of the transit planning firms telling me in the strongest terms that I was interfering with their business. So then was The Aerospace Corporation, the Executive Office of the President, the Minnesota Legislature, and numerous others. The fact that it had been shown that deploying only conventional transit would not relieve congestion, but that PRT had the potential to do so mattered not at all. The concern was not about what would be good for the nation as a whole, but what would make the greatest near-term profits for a relatively few persons possessed of the right kind of influence.

By offering funds for conventional rail systems, notwithstanding their inefficiency and inability to compete with the automobile, government had distorted an otherwise free market. The market is still distorted. If states or cities had to find their own funds to build transit systems, the situation would be far different. It is unfortunate that city planners have become accustomed to looking to the federal government for grants to plan and to deploy inefficient systems, notwithstanding detailed economic arguments by federal, as well as other, economists.

The belief of rail fans that conventional rail is **the** answer and that thoughts of superior new systems are only a "will-o'-the-wisp" is very strong and very emotional. A problem is that transit is a complex quantitative subject. Much data must be examined, yet too many people look for simple solutions. It takes a special learning experience to fully understand the differences between new and conventional transit systems, and it has become fashionable to prevent comparisons.

Fortunately, the Chicago RTA initiative in PRT has partially broken through the wall built to keep PRT out of the picture. In addition to Chicago, federally sponsored studies in the U. S. are underway in Seattle and Rhode Island. The fact that federal ISTEA funds can be used for transit projects at the discretion of states is, under present circumstances, a key to progress. My recommendation to cities is that they propose planning and *design* studies of new transit applications; such has been done recently in Sweden.

The planning portion of such a study determines line and station locations, does operations analysis, performs ridership analysis, and makes economic comparisons of alternatives. The design portion related to new systems does computer simulations of moving vehicles across flexible spans in which vehicle weight, speed, and span length are varied to determine optimum vehicle weight, optimum span length, and minimum guideway size and weight; it determines the size, layout, and performance desired of vehicles; develops virtual-reality videos to gain impressions of the visual impact of the system; gathers available information on the required control system; and recommends suppliers. With the backing of a responsible entity, such as an MPO, responsible suppliers will appear and the cycle of inaction can be broken.

My recommendation is that only if the community in open

hearings becomes satisfied with the capital and operating costs, the performance, and the visual impact of the preferred alternative should they proceed, and then only if they can do so on their own funds. I see no sound reason why general taxation over the entire country should fund projects of benefit to only one local area. If any federal funds are to be provided, they should be for research and development only. Present practices promote the worst of pork-barrel politics. The capital grants program should be abolished. It promotes waste, it corrupts the market, and it makes liars out of otherwise nice people.

Appendix B

The Birth of a Breakthrough in Urban Transportation

J. Edward Anderson
North Park College Chapel Lecture
Chicago, Illinois
March 1, 1994

Abstract

The author was invited to speak at North Park College as the 1994 Distinguished Alumnus Lecturer on his role in the development of Personal Rapid Transit (PRT), the first genuinely new urban transportation system to appear in a century. This Chapel Lecture describes his relevant technical experience, his search for meaning, his need for interdisciplinary project work, and the extraordinary circumstances and timing that led him to PRT as a new career, and that carried this work to the point where it has been taken over by a major corporation and a major urban transportation authority. The lecture ends with a challenge to young people to aim high and seek a noble cause of fundamental importance to mankind.

An Aerospace Career

I am a mechanical engineer. There were no adults in our early lives that influenced my brother Ray and me into the field of engineering, but both of us knew by about the age of 12 that we were going to be engineers. There were warnings in books on careers that after the war was over (WWII in this case), there would be few opportunities in engineering. Yet, we never thought in terms of any other vocation.

I have now practiced and taught mechanical engineering for almost 45 years. I have known engineers who wished they had taken up a different profession. This has not been so in my case. I can't say I have enjoyed every minute of it, there have been difficult times, but on the whole my career has been exciting for me and varied—never, or hardly ever, a dull moment.

I spent the first third of my career in aerospace engineering. Green, with a Bachelor's Degree in Mechanical Engineering from Iowa State University, I was hired by the Structures Research Laboratory at NACA, the National Advisory Committee for Aeronautics, predecessor to NASA, at Langley Field, Virginia. There I developed methods for calculating stresses and deflections in supersonic aircraft wings and received the equivalent of a Master's Degree on the job.

After a few years, I moved to the Honeywell Aeronautical Division in Minneapolis, where, a course at a time with no time off and no reimbursement for tuition, I earned a real MSME from the University of Minnesota. My mother had urged me many times to get all the education I could, and I wanted to take her advice.

At the Aero Division at the age of 25 I was given a budget of $35,000 a month and single-handedly designed an aircraft fuel gage sensor that left Honeywell with no competitors. I was then asked to do the mechanical design of the first transistorized amplifier that flew in a U. S. military aircraft and in so doing was the first at Honeywell to introduce printed circuits, nylon gearing, and adhesive bonding. The design won the Aviation Age Product of the Month Award.

Looking for new worlds to conquer, I transferred to engineering research on autopilots for fighter aircraft and missiles as a research engineer and manager of the work of about 15 engineers during some of the peak years of the post-Korean-War military build-up.

After a couple of years, I was invited to move to the field of inertial navigation, where I invented and led the development of a new type of inertial navigation. I had the recent satisfaction of learning that my work on so-called "gimballess inertial navigation" has been incorporated into laser-inertial guidance packages that now fly aboard almost every commercial aircraft.

A New Challenge

On October 4, 1957 the Soviet Union launched its first Sputnik spacecraft. It was a tiny device by the standards of the next decade, but it was a wake-up call, a challenge to American scientific and engineering prowess. It brought on the new math that tormented many children, but for me it created a challenge.

Right after Sputnik, the Aero Division Director of Planning proclaimed that there should be more Ph.D.s in the Honeywell Aeronautical Research Department, where I worked. I had wanted to get a Ph.D. but by then had just about given up on the idea. I thought about it until the summer of 1958 when I decided to go for it. That was the best decision of my professional life! It opened up avenues essential to my later work in directions I could not have dreamed possible.

By June 1959 I was at work in a Ph.D. program in the Department of Aeronautics and Astronautics at M. I. T., the greatest engineering school in the world, starting one of the most enjoyable phases of an enjoyable career. I wanted to broaden my understanding of physics and mathematics and generally wanted to broaden my knowledge base, thinking at the time in purely technical terms.

I wanted to explore exciting new fields. I spent most of the first year studying the Special and General Theories of Relativity, and even solved the clock paradox problem in General Relativity. But, as time went on, I realized that I had to be practical, and my search for the right field of study led me to magnetohydrodynamics, which is the study of the interaction between conducting gases and magnetic fields. It promised the hope of substantially more efficient electric power, and required the learning of a lot of physics and math that interested me. I finished in late 1961 with a thesis entitled "Magnetohydrodynamic Shock Waves" that was the only one of 200 M. I. T. Ph.D. theses published that year by The M. I. T. Press. It was later republished by the University of Tokyo Press and in Russian by a Moscow publisher Atomizdat.

At that stage of my life, I didn't think there was anything I couldn't master if I set my mind to it. But, I had to go back to work at Honeywell to earn a living.

A Search for Meaning

With my new background, I was assigned to manage a 25-man team to do the advanced design of an unmanned Solar Probe, a spacecraft that was to go within the orbit of Mercury to gather data on fields and particles around the sun.

The project led to Honeywell's first spacecraft contract, an infrared probe that flew around the earth. I found that the hardest part of the Solar Probe project, which I took on personally, was to justify the mission. NASA even called later to ask permission to use my report in their Congressional testimony to justify their missions. Rather than being flattered, I was troubled. I wanted to be relevant.

I also had a burning desire to be an educator, so in 1963, I left a promising career in military and space engineering for a professorship in Mechanical Engineering at the University of Minnesota. I soon realized, however, that there was a cost in uprooting one's self from an environment in which one's capabilities were understood and appreciated. Now I was "low man on the totem pole." I had to work my way up all over again, although in an exciting field made possible for me by my research at M. I. T.

During the 1960s the United States and the Soviet Union had a scientific-exchange program involving 30 professors each year. I was offered an opportunity to participate. It was a good time for me personally, so I accepted and spent the period from November 1967 through August 1968 as a guest of the Soviet Academy of Sciences mostly in Minsk, but for periods in Moscow, Leningrad, and ten other Soviet cities.

I had interesting adventures, but most importantly I had time to read broadly and to contemplate the direction of my career. I was very concerned that my work be enjoyable, meaningful, and worth the expenditure of my time. I was in a hurry and I felt time slipping by. Frankly, I was undergoing a serious mid-life crisis.

I read many books while in Minsk, the most influential of which was a volume of writings of Thomas Jefferson. My most important realization from reading Jefferson was that he was always talking about the first-rank problems of his time. Why couldn't I also work on a first-rank problem of my time? Was it possible for an engineer to work on first-rank problems?

Some time during that period of quiet a most meaningful statement of Jesus came to me: "He who shall lose his life for my sake shall find it and find it in abundance." I interpreted that to mean, "He who shall become deeply involved in a cause of fundamental need for mankind shall find his life in abundance."

That was it! The purpose of life is service in the best way each individual can provide that service.

New Directions

Being aware of my successes at Honeywell and M.I.T., I had the confidence to aim high. I concluded that the most enjoyable, meaningful, worthwhile work that I, as an engineer, could do could not involve becoming more and more highly specialized in a narrow field such as I was in, but it would be interdisciplinary, it would involve systems engineering in the broadest sense. Unfortunately for me, Universities were organized around highly specialized individuals, each encouraged to deepen his or her specialized knowledge.

I read an article by a University of Michigan professor who commented that the important problems of the day were interdisciplinary. They were falling neglected in the cracks between the disciplines. A rank ordering of problems of importance began with trying to prevent nuclear war, then doing something about the burgeoning environmental problems, problems of civil rights and of poverty, and so on. He concluded that the vast majority of university faculty were working on problems of about the tenth to the twelfth order in importance, almost the equivalent of Nero fiddling while Rome burned.

By the established system of recognition, faculty members were discouraged from the kind of interdisciplinary work that would raise the rank order of importance of the problems they worked on to something close the Jeffersonian ideal.

I sent a 16-page handwritten letter to my Department Head explaining all of my reasons for my belief that I couldn't find what I needed at a University. I offered my resignation, not realizing what a terrible time it was for an aerospace engineer to find any job, much less a meaningful one. The Apollo Moon Program was ending, and Aerospace engineers were being laid off by the thousands. My Department Head, Dr. Richard Jordan, wrote back and said "Don't resign, I think I have something here that would appeal to you."

Upon returning, he handed me a solicitation from the newly formed Urban Mass Transportation Administration inviting Universities to submit interdisciplinary proposals to study the application of new technologies to problems of urban transportation. I had not thought a microsecond about the possibility of working in urban transportation, but the descriptions I read of the possibilities of new personal transit systems sounded appealing and would enable me to apply knowledge and skills I had acquired in every phase of my career.

Urban Transportation

I had experienced the worsening problems of transportation during the 1950s and 1960s. The whole urban environment was becoming more and more profoundly and negatively influenced by automobiles. Autos were so convenient that virtually everyone wanted one. Credit had become so easy that virtually everyone could afford one. Street congestion was becoming a major concern as more and more people abandoned the bus, streetcar and train for the auto. In Wintertime, while tediously making my way in my car through Minneapolis in a foot of snow, sliding around, stopping and starting, waiting for traffic, I had wondered if there wasn't a better way. Now, with a possible solution presented to me, a better way was no longer a fantasy. The federal government was backing research!

I had watched beautiful green lawns, bushes, flower gardens and trees give way to asphalt parking lots. I saw that the increasing rush of autos made street parking hopelessly inadequate, leading to huge, expensive multi-story parking structures.

One particular street in Minneapolis had beautiful 100-year-old elm trees on its boulevards for many miles. Well before Dutch-elm decease was a problem, these trees were all cut down to widen the street by one lane, and in the process the beautiful character of that community was destroyed. Although I didn't live near that street, I had a feeling of great loss. Could this, I thought, be progress?

More and more roads and streets were being designed just for the automobile, with no thought for sidewalks or bicycle paths. As downtown streets widened at the expense of narrower sidewalks, the attractiveness of downtowns gradually declined. With more and more ground covered by asphalt and concrete, there was less room for grass, trees and flower gardens. Asphalt and concrete absorb and reradiate the sun's energy and significantly warm the city in summertime. Living plants also absorb the sun's energy; but, in the process of photosynthesis, they hold much of that energy and release it as heat only in autumn as the leaves decay. The result is a significant reduction in summertime temperatures. Is there any wonder that people moved farther and farther out in the suburbs to find comfort, solitude, green grass and trees?

I had witnessed terrible battles over the introduction of urban freeways, which of course went through the poorer communities where the political resistance was the least. Once built these freeways divided neighborhoods and destroyed community spirit. The noise was so intense that 20-foot walls had to be built next to them, and property values declined drastically for the unfortunate people whose houses were next to the freeway rights of way but were not taken.

We learned about lead poisoning from auto exhausts. We saw the levels of carbon monoxide and hydrocarbons rise and affect our health. We saw mothers spending too much time as chauffeur while the children were young, and then watched our children reach driving age and work too many hours in menial jobs earning money to buy a car, barely having time to enjoy it because of the time required to earn the payments. We saw our city bus companies go broke and we saw them replaced by inefficient bureaucracies.

I read a broad-based interdisciplinary study by General Research Corporation of Santa Barbara, California, that examined the future of cities if only conventional transit systems were deployed, and compared that future with the future if the new personal transit systems were deployed. The conclusion, reported in the July 1969 issue of Scientific American, was that congestion would continually worsen if only conventional transit systems were deployed, but that congestion could be arrested if personal transit systems were widely deployed.

A New Career

In the Fall of 1968, with colleagues from several departments at the University of Minnesota, I plunged enthusiastically into work on a grant proposal on Research and Training in new forms of urban transportation. We won a grant, and that enabled us to get a serious start in this new venture.

While engaged in learning all I could about personal transit, later called "personal rapid transit" or PRT, I began studying and lecturing about environmental issues generally. In the Spring Term of 1970, the Spring of the first Earth Day, my colleagues and I inaugurated an interdisciplinary course we called "Ecology, Technology and Society." During preparation to moderate this course, I converted from a person concerned about environmental problems but from the sidelines, to an activist. I saw the consequences of too many automobiles as the major deterrent to an acceptable urban environment, and PRT to be the only reasonable way to turn a deteriorating situation around.

I had been looking for a hard problem; a meaningful, relevant, hard problem. I decided to devote my career to the problem of implementation of PRT, how to make it actually happen.

That was an unusual type of problem for a University Professor to take on. I realized the risks, but had tenure, and decided that I had to ignore the reward system if I was to "lose my life" in a cause worth pursuing.

Enter the RTA

I had no idea that it would take two decades of hard, persistent work before a major transit agency would become interested. In Spring 1989, the leadership of the Northern Illinois Regional Transportation Authority (the RTA) concluded that they could not solve their transportation problems in the Chicago Area with only more roads and more conventional rail systems. One of them commented: "there must be a rocket scientist out there with an idea that can help us."

We met them a month later, and that meeting has now, five years later, grown into a contract between the RTA and Raytheon Company involving a commitment of almost $40 million to design and test a PRT system along the lines we had, since 1982, been developing. This has taken great courage on the part of the RTA Board. If they succeed, they will have realized one of the greatest technologies of the declining years of the Twentieth Century. With only century-old transit concepts deployed, congestion has since 1969, as predicted, worsened substantially.

Divine Guidance

How we got to where we are today has involved enough uncanny, seemingly lucky coincidences to fill a book, which we hope to write once PRT is in operation, and have convinced us that we must have been blessed with Divine Guidance. It was right for PRT to be brought through an incredible labyrinth of challenges and pitfalls over two decades to the point it is today, a few years from operational reality.

I mentioned early in this lecture my background in engineering to comment here that my sequence of experiences was crucial to giving me the engineering know-how, discipline, and confidence that I could succeed, notwithstanding all of the naysayers that have appeared along the way. There was no way for me to know in the 1950s and 1960s where my work would lead, but in looking back, every phase contributed something I would need in the design of a new PRT system. There was no way for me to know then that PRT could not have been developed by governments because they require too much consensus too soon, and it could not have been developed by industries because they require too early a return on investment. PRT could only be developed in a Research University.

The Human Mind

Technical education and experience alone were not enough! Equally, and perhaps more importantly, were the lessons learned from books and hard knocks about dealing with people. Everything we do, whether it be in dealing with the physical world or not, involves interaction of people, individually or in various types of organizations. Those who say that engineers deal only with things while others deal with people cannot have had much experience in real engineering. I give lectures every year on the psychology of engineering and creativity in engineering, and I regard these topics as essential as all of the technical topics. They involve the relationship between the right brain and the left brain; how to take advantage of the capabilities of both sides of your brain.

From the last century to the present, there has been a profound advance in understanding of the workings of the human mind, and of its affect on the physical body, its own and others. Having said this, I must hasten to add that my observations and reading have convince me that we are on the threshold of a quantum leap in further practical understanding of the power of the mind over events.

If everyone could be trained in this knowledge, how much greater would be our prosperity and our tranquillity. Many minds of a century ago carried resentments, anger, hatred, anguish over past events, and bitterness to the point of destroying effectiveness and ruining lives. Even outstanding scientists let the acid of hatred lead to tragic lives and early death. Of course this happens all too frequently today. Not everyone reads the psychological literature.

Destructive behavior has been countered by wise counsel of religious leaders to love one's enemies, to forgive, and to forget. But, all too often we resolve, after a Sunday morning sermon, to improve, but by Monday morning fall back into our old habits. Today more and more leaders of mind-body research add hard-headed scientific evidence that love, forgiveness and prayer really work. One must harbor no resentments. One must cleanse one's mind of all negative thoughts, which are destructive not only of one's relations to others, but affect, often disastrously, one's own health.

New Challenges

Are there new challenges for young people today?

We live in an age of mounting problems. The world faces practically unconstrained population growth, with an additional billion people expected in only six or seven years; with the prospect of one hundred million more people in the United States in two decades. We have waste disposal problems that now force states to ship wastes thousands of miles to dump sites at heretofore-unimaginable costs.

We have a burden of debt with interest that now consumes 57% of our income taxes, and with the need to borrow more money just to pay the interest. And this is not static. With present policies, in a decade that 57% could, if we lack determination, be ruinously higher, leaving our children and grandchildren with staggering reminders of our fiscal irresponsibility.

We all know that problems of crime are increasing. We are reminded continuously that our educational system is not adequate, and that we are falling behind. We know that we have too many people caught, with apparent permanence, in structural poverty. We know that our health-care system cannot continue as it is, but there is not enough consensus as to appropriate remedies. We are faced with the prospect of potentially disastrous climate change due to relentless increases in dumping of carbon dioxide and other substances into the atmosphere. We fear the loss of the rain forests and the further effect that will have on our climate.

With respect to urban transportation, urban settlements everywhere are crying for solutions. PRT is an essential element, but most planners and opinion leaders will do nothing until it is demonstrated. PRT has been referred to as an essential technology of a sustainable world. But, we are not out of the woods yet. There are many pitfalls and there is too little understanding. Your help, your positive thoughts, and your prayers are much needed.

Every one of these problems requires for its solution, interdisciplinary, systematic thinking. Yet far too many brilliant scientists still concentrate on narrow specialties and leave interdisciplinary work to others. We do need specialists, but we need a balance between specialists and interdisciplinarians. Fortunately, more and more colleges and universities are recognizing the importance of interdisciplinary research as a respected academic discipline, and the National Science Foundation is now funding such research.

Are there new challenges for young people today?

You bet there are! Are you preparing for a significant role in the solutions? Do you think you can contribute in a significant way? Don't underestimate what you, as one individual, can do. With dedication, concentration, careful study, carefully prepared papers, thoughtful speeches, and a burning desire to make a difference, you can and will make a difference.

The world is full of cynics and naysayers who will put logs in your path, who will discourage you at every step. Be ready to understand them and to answer them calmly, kindly, factually, with respect, and with love in your heart. Your challenge, with tact and perseverance, is to prevail.

Remember the advice of Jesus: "He who shall lose his life for my sake shall find it and find it in abundance."

Acknowledgments

Because of limitations on time, I have mentioned only one person in this lecture, yet the current state of development of PRT has been reached only because of the dedicated work of many dozens of individuals who preceded us, who joined us, and who worked in parallel with us. Their essential work must be acknowledged in a history of development of PRT. Without them, this story could not have been written.

$\mathscr{A}ppendix\ C$

Partial Biography—Railroad Experience of A. Scheffer Lang

Denver & Rio Grande Western Railroad—Operating officer

U. S. Army Transportation Corps—Instructor in railway maintenance and operations

New York Central Railroad—Director of Operating Data Systems

U. S. Department of Commerce—Deputy Undersecretary for Transportation Research

U. S. Department of Transportation—Federal Railroad Administrator

Massachusetts Institute of Technology—Professor of Civil Engineering, Head of the Transportation Systems Division—Department of Civil Engineering

Association of American Railroads—Assistant to the President for Staff Studies

Soo Line Railroad—Vice President, Executive Department.

Printed in the United States
4286